The

Laws

of

Hope

The Light is Here

Ryuho Okawa

IRH PRESS

BOOKS
IRH PRESS
New York

ISBN 13: 978-1-942125-76-1
ISBN 10: 1-942125-76-3

Printed in Canada

First Edition

Cover Design: Jess Morphew
Cover Image: berya113/Getty Images

Contents

PROLOGUE

On Hope

How Your Hopes Come True

CHAPTER ONE

Try to Praise Yourself More

Getting Rid of a Bad Self-Image

CHAPTER TWO

What It Means to Succeed

Success Principles We Don't Learn in School

CHAPTER THREE

Success That Prevails from This World to the Other World

Hints for Understanding The Laws of Success

CHAPTER FOUR

Becoming Invincible
How Organizations' Leaders Need to Think

CHAPTER FIVE

Fulfill Your Mission of Light

Filling This Earth with Light

Preface

This book is the core essence of modern religion. In this book, *The Laws of Hope*, the foundation of the modern Laws of salvation is now set down. I've dared to lay down all modern self-help teachings, while knowing all about the saving power of belief in another power.

I am the Light, the One who came down to this world to shed light on all of you. This person, I, is teaching the Laws of hope for lighting yourselves up. I wish for you to know the delight of lighting yourself up. I wish for you to be enlightened about the reason you were born to this world.

Happiness and success shall be in everyone's grasp. It's my reason for creating Happy Science. Japan is, indeed, in need of the Buddha now. And the Light of Truth that's shedding light on the world is now here.

Ryuho Okawa
Master and CEO of Happy Science Group
January 1, 2006

PROLOGUE

On Hope

How Your Hopes Come True

1

Basic Ways of Thinking to Make Your Hopes Come True

Is Your Hope Right for You?

I would like to talk about your hopes. Your hopes coming true is generally believed to be happiness, itself, coming true. Therefore, at Happy Science also, the idea of your hopes coming true is considered very important for achieving the happiness you are seeking.

Actually, in some sense, the hopes you hold in your heart express who you are as a person. In another sense, your hopes, or what you are wishing to achieve from the bottom of your heart, set the course of your life's destiny. This means that looking at your hopes will show you your destiny.

On top of that, we can say that this wish is, indeed, connected to your essence if your hopes are not just temporary or superficial, if the wish in your heart that says, "When I think of my life, I can't help wishing I could be this way," comes up from the depths of your being again and again, over a long course of time.

So, the first thing to examine is whether your hope is right for you. Whether your hope will come true depends first on this point. If your hope is right for you, then, of course, your aim to make it come true is heading in a good direction and will not harm others. The high spirits of the heavenly world also won't hesitate to assist you. So, first, it's essential to always examine whether your thoughts or wishes are right for you.

Is Your Hope Right for Your Mindset and Efforts?

I have written in various books, so far, that your thoughts do not immediately become reality in this world, and instead, they take time to do so. On the other hand, they immediately become reality in the other world. I've often given this teaching in this way. But if I were to explain more precisely, I would say that there are thoughts that will become reality in the other world, but there are also ones that won't.

What do I mean? If it were exactly as I've been saying, if it were truly as I've been writing it—that your thoughts immediately become reality in the other world—then the spirits of Hell would immediately be able to escape when they wished to do so. By just wishing to go up to Heaven, they would be able to go there immediately. By just wishing to become an angel, they would become one immediately. But, in reality, things don't work out so easily.

Then, how about the spirits in Heaven? Can someone who has died and gone back to the other world just recently, who is not used to it yet, become an angel immediately by wishing to do so? It's also not so simple in this case. To be an angel, you need the spiritual training and capacity of an angel. So becoming an angel is a good aim to have, but in reality, you have to fulfill certain conditions in order to become one.

On the other hand, could an angel become the Devil in Hell, as soon as he or she aimed to do so? This, also, would not be so easy to do. If you are an angel, you have maintained a good heart over a long course of time and you have lived by a life principle of not having the heart of the Devil. So, like an actor, you could pretend to be the Devil in Hell for a short period. But it would be very difficult to spend a long time living as the Devil. It would be very difficult living a long time in that way, the same way a land-dwelling animal cannot breathe or live underwater and a water-dwelling creature cannot live on top of the land.

What do I mean? What I mean is the following: It's often said that your thoughts become reality, your wishes come true, and your hopes get fulfilled, but we should say more precisely that they become fulfilled or become reality in the way that's suited to who you are. Or, if I were to put it in terms of the Buddhist law of cause and effect—that is, the teaching that a cause leads to a result, that good deeds lead to good outcomes and bad deeds lead to bad outcomes—then I should say that your hopes attract the result that is best suited to your mindset.

Living in this world, what you're hoping for might be extremely far from who you are presently. Because of this, your hope doesn't become reality, which makes you worry. Or the opposite of your hope might have come true. But with regard to your hopes getting realized, the outcome that's best suited to your mindset will indeed appear.

The outcome best suited to who you are as a person, your efforts, or your talent will appear. If your thoughts and their outcomes differ a lot from each other, if you get an outcome that you didn't expect, it usually means that you are not correctly seeing who you currently are—you are not seeing your efforts, self-reflection, talents, and human relationships correctly.

If what you are wishing for is suitable for you, if you deserve to see your wish come true because of your way of life and your efforts, if it's suitable for your wish to come true because of who you are, even as seen by other people and angels, then your wish surely will come true. It might occur either quickly or slowly in terms of this earthly world's time, but it will definitely become a reality.

If your wish doesn't come true, this means either that your wish was not right for you or that your wish coming true was not suitable for you at this time. So, if your strong wish doesn't come true, first please check to see whether it's a right hope for you to have, and, in addition to that, please check whether it's suitable for your mindset and efforts. Please think deeply about these two points. The gap that you recognize indicates the areas of life you should review and make further efforts to improve.

Your Hopes Are Being Considered from a Standpoint Beyond Human Understanding

I will add that while we are living in this earthly world, we see things based on this third-dimensional world and our physical lives. And because we do, we're not able to see through everything perfectly, even if we are very exceptional people. No matter how hard we try, there are times when we cannot see through everything, because we are limited as finite human beings. In such cases, we shouldn't try to judge the results without seeing the outcome over a much longer period, past this current life.

Therefore, you should also know that there is a consideration from a larger standpoint that is beyond human understanding. You might believe that your hope is a suitable outcome for you, but from the much, much higher standpoint of God's or Buddha's designs, in some cases, He can clearly see that a different course or a different outcome would be better for your life. In such cases, it's important to accept that outcome with grace.

2

The Essentials of Your Hopes Coming True

Aim for Sacred Self-Realization through Prayer

I've now talked about the basic ways of thinking behind your hopes coming true.

When your hopes come true, it is, indeed, a basic happiness. As long as we live as human beings, we, indeed, want to have hopes and dreams. And we, indeed, want them to come true. Therefore, it's essential to make daily efforts while hoping that your hopes are right for you and that Heaven and other people will accept them. Then, as you live your life as who you are, there might be times when you just cannot see the road ahead of you. You might feel lost, and you might suffer. You will probably go through times of such suffering that you don't know what to seek—times when, in your anguish, you don't know what to aim for. There is no one who doesn't go through such a time in their life. So, when you come to your limit, when you feel lost, when you don't know what path to take and are suffering, when you become broken-spirited, when you painfully recognize the limitations of this physical life, please pray. Prayer is, indeed, the first and last measure given to you.

Aim for sacred self-realization through prayer. When you pray, accept, with peace in your mind, the outcome that appears to you. Your righteous prayers will definitely be heard. People have been given this great power. When you are in adversity and you can do nothing more by yourself or by your own strength, you are able to discover prayer.

To achieve your hopes, take the final step of praying. If you don't think you can make them come true by yourself, gather the strength and hearts of many people together and pray. For when you do, the outcome that is suited to you will definitely appear. And so, having the mindset to peacefully accept this outcome is important.

Courage and Wisdom
Are Also Essential

Up to now, I have talked about the following things regarding your hopes: your hopes should be right for you, you must accept the outcome that appears as the one that's suited to you, you must accept the changes and adjustments made from a standpoint beyond human understanding, and, finally, use prayer when the path does not seem to open to you no matter what you do. Prayer will definitely save you.

I want to add, as the very final path, that courage and wisdom are also necessary for your hopes to come true. If your hope doesn't come true, it's asking you whether you have courage, whether you have wisdom, whether you have used up all the wisdom inside you. Please don't forget these things.

Make prayer a basic aspect of your life, and please don't forget that courage and wisdom are also essential for your hopes to come true. When you do these things, a fire will light up in your heart, and before long it will light up the world. This is how your hopes will come true.

Though I have spoken very simply, this is the prologue to this book, *The Laws of Hope*.

CHAPTER ONE

.˙٭˙.

Try to
Praise Yourself More

Getting Rid of a Bad Self-Image

1 ·

Depressed Feelings Have Become Widespread in Society

In a Depressive Condition,
You Are Always Thinking Negatively about Yourself

In this chapter, I would like to talk about the theme "Try to Praise Yourself More." I don't usually write about this kind of theme. It's a theme that I haven't lectured on before. So, why am I teaching about this now? I feel that modern society is highly competitive and stressful, and as an outgrowth of that, depressed feelings have become widespread in our society. For a long time, insecure, low-spirited, disheartened, downhearted feelings have been around, and the economic recession over the past decade or so has made things worse.

When depressed feelings are so widespread, the number of suicides increases. Every year, more than thirty thousand people in Japan commit suicide, and an even greater number of people must be on the verge of doing so—this number could be tenfold or even a hundredfold the number of actual suicides. Also, because depressed feelings affect our health in various ways, both mentally and physically, even in people who are not suicidal, I feel that it has led to the strains, problems, and sufferings of society itself.

What are the symptoms of depression like? The most familiar example is the way we feel during the rainy season. In Japan, on rainy days in June, the weather is very clammy every day. When this season comes, we feel so miserable. Humidity is terribly high, and it rains constantly. Eighty percent of office workers wish they didn't have to leave for work, and children become reluctant to go to school. We experience this kind of phenomenon of depressed feelings during the rainy season. But actually, I've recognized such symptoms of chronic depression or conditions close to that in an increasing number of people, even during the drier seasons.

Over the past 20 years, I have taught a lot about self-reflection. When depressed people practice self-reflection, it goes well in some cases, of course, but I've noticed that it doesn't in very many cases. Sometimes, depressed people treat themselves more and more severely as they continue to practice. When they practice a lot of self-reflection, sometimes they end up telling themselves that they are completely worthless, that they are complete nobodies. If you are like them, you might lose all your will to go on, and actually, you could even feel the urge to commit suicide.

So, before practicing self-reflection, it's important to look carefully at the condition of your mind. Even in the medical world, patients suffering from clinical levels of depression receive treatment that's not so different from religious methods, since the doctors need to provide them with some kind of prescription.

In a depressive condition, you are full of negative thoughts about yourself. You are thinking, "This was wrong with me and that was wrong, too. Looking back, everything about me has been wrong for a long time. The problems began a long time ago. This was a bad thing, and that was a bad thing, too." For some people, it was their parents' occupations or small incomes that were bad. For others, it was not having any brothers or sisters—or the opposite, having too many siblings. Then there are the various levels of school people go to, such as college, high school, and junior high school. For some people, it was bad that they couldn't get into a certain school, or contrary to that, it was bad they got accepted into that school, because later on they were defeated by the competition there.

The same thing is true regarding the companies people work for. Some people believe their life is bad because they weren't hired by a good company, while others blame it on working at a good company. It's the same regarding marriages. While some people regret not getting married, many other people blame their marriage for what happened to their life. Many people feel that their family life got complicated when they got married, and regret having gotten married. Some people regret not having had any children, but others believe that their children are the reason for what happened to their life. Looking back over your past in this way, you can find many causes of your misfortune, and when you look upon yourself at this moment, everything looks negative. Many people must find themselves in such a situation. In Japan alone, there are more than several million such people, probably tens of millions of them. Most likely, a significant number of people are in this situation.

With such types of people, if they practice self-reflection the right way they will be fine, but if they don't, they can go further into depression, so we require another level of thinking. I thought about these things and decided to give the following teachings on the theme "Try to Praise Yourself More."

See Whether Your Miserable Self-Image Is Objectively True

When you are feeling depressed and always being hard on yourself, other people will empathize with you and you will seem a very pure person in their eyes, in some sense. It is the kind of situation we usually read about in novels. Characters are portrayed in situations like yours, making the novels interesting to read. Seeing the main character and other characters go through that kind of suffering, seeing them suffering inner pain and misery that hurts them to their stomachs, readers feel empathy, and when they finish the novel, they say how good it was.

Objectively speaking, however, for the actual person, it is not so easy to be in this kind of situation. Please look objectively at how you have been thinking negatively about yourself all the time and being hard on yourself. Is it correct to look at yourself this way? To other people's objective eyes, from the viewpoint of everyone in society, in the eyes of all humankind, or in the eyes of God, is it correct to keep finding flaws in yourself? In a state of depression, you will easily find 10 or 20 reasons why you are a failure. If you speak about these reasons, it will result in complaining. But, from an objective standpoint, is the substance of what you are saying really true? I don't think many people in this state of mind have looked very far into this point. Probably, fewer than one in ten people, or maybe fewer than one in a hundred people have.

If you are feeling depressed, you could be shrinking inwardly, thinking you are a good-for-nothing person. You could have a miserable, unresilient, poor self-image. You could have the self-image of a drenched dog. But if you could detach from yourself and look closely at yourself, you would realize that something about this self-image is not completely correct. You could be just desiring things you cannot have or magnifying the things you do not have enough of. You could be forgetting what you already have now or have already been given. You could be looking in this way at a lot of things.

In this way, you might believe that you are looking at yourself objectively, but in truth, you have only been seeing things from your current viewpoint. Your view is different depending on whether you're going uphill or downhill on a roller coaster, and you might only be looking at yourself through the eyes of someone screaming in terror. You might not be looking at yourself from any other viewpoint. In some cases, another person can serve as your objective eye and give you counseling and advice, saying, "What in the world are you saying? You think that about yourself, but you're not like that at all; you're like this." If you are blessed with good friends like that, in some cases, you can find some kind of salvation.

All in all, when we are suffering from depression, we think of everything negatively. We have various thoughts like, "This marriage was a mistake, so I have to get a divorce," "Getting this job was a mistake, so I have to quit and get another job somewhere else," or "This happened to me because I moved here, so I have to sell this house and move somewhere else."

2

Why People Become Depressed

Depression Is Caused by Your Environment Changing Due to Such Events as a Job Transfer or Getting Married

It is said that people's depression often results from their environment changing. For example, an Osaka-raised businessperson could be working in his city and then suddenly get transferred to Tokyo for the first time in his life. From the outside, this looks like an advancement in his position. People around him are congratulating him. But inside himself, he is thinking, "I have never lived in Tokyo before. I've only visited there once, on a school trip, and there were so many people there that I nearly got lost. I wish I didn't have to move there." These are his feelings, but meanwhile, the people around him are congratulating him and giving him a going-away party. So, on the surface, he says to them, "I am so glad. Maybe this will help me become successful," when, in actuality, he is gradually becoming depressed.

It's a situation that does, indeed, happen. I'm certain that many people have gone through this kind of experience. Even though others think that you should be happy about your situation, you worry about whether you can adapt to the new environment, and you get depressed.

Getting married is also an event to be happy about, but some people vanish into thin air the day before their wedding. They back down out of fear, feeling unbearable pressure and nerves. It is hard to go from living alone to living with someone else around the clock. It would be strange, frankly speaking, if it didn't make you feel tremendous pressure. After you've passed the age of 20, even living with your parents would be difficult. That was only possible when you were a child. If you had to be around them all the time, you would end up fighting all the time. This is true of your siblings, too: after a certain age, you would have conflicts with them all the time if you had to live together.

There is even bigger pressure if you're entering an arranged marriage and are about to marry someone you've just met only recently. But even in a love marriage, you might have seen each other just a few times. While some couples spend time seeing each other for five or ten years before getting married, most commonly, people only date two or three years before getting married. So when you imagine living around the clock with this person, having children, building a family, and spending four or five decades of your life together until death, suddenly you feel uncertain, and the pressure becomes unbearable. Some people come to feel this way and change their minds or back out just before their wedding ceremony or as soon as they come home from the wedding. In the end, it's because of the pressure they feel about changing their way of living.

So sometimes we feel pressure when we move to a new environment, for example when we are transferred to another part of our company. Marriage is another event in life that can put a lot of pressure on us. Compared with our lives before it, the stress that we feel is multiplied twofold or threefold.

Also, if it's about your marriage only, maybe spending your life with your spouse would be fine for you, but you might go into depression once you have a child. This is because for some time while you're still young and newly wedded, your job will keep you very busy. Things could have been going smoothly in your life with just each other. But when a child comes, it can be very difficult. Children are like creatures of the unknown. They cannot be controlled in any way. They will move around, cry, demand things, become hungry, or get sick, not minding their parents' needs. This is why some people who have children quickly fall into depression.

This could happen with your first child, your second child, or your third child. A point comes when your ability, or your capacity, gets overburdened. So, if your married life is causing you some struggles already, your capacity will get overwhelmed when you have a child.

Also, in some cases, it will be the wife who gets depressed. Some women try to be a good wife and work hard to take care of their husband, but once the baby comes, they're not able to take care of both. They have to take care of the baby and neglect their husband.

But this then invites complaints from their husband. If they try to give their husband and baby equal attention, they will end up being terrible at both. But if they give up giving attention to their baby, this could have tough consequences, also, later on. Without enough love from their parents, children are apt to become delinquent or have various other kinds of problems.

In this way, objectively, getting married ought to be celebrated, and having a child ought to be praised, but they bring additional pressure all of a sudden, and people might fall into a depression. This is something many people experience.

The Fear of Facing
Unknown Experiences

Earlier, I talked about depression caused by getting transferred to another post at work. Depression can also be caused by being promoted. You might have complaints as someone in a basic employee's position who never seems to get promoted. But, for example, if you were ever promoted to a manager's position and eight people were placed under you, you might suddenly become depressed, thinking to yourself, "This is going to be tough. How do I manage my subordinates? I'm not sure what kind of thinking and what kind of abilities I'll need. How do I get my subordinates to do good work?" So far, you've only needed to do your own work. You have never before had to produce results by managing others. So you might fall into a depression. You never learned in school how to manage subordinates. Even though school taught you how to study, it never taught you about how to manage people to produce results. You've never in your life done this yourself nor ever watched how someone else did.

If you grew up in a household that incidentally runs a family business, many employees were around you, so you probably spent your childhood watching your parents manage people. If this was the case for you, you might be somewhat capable of managing people. But if you never watched the way your parents worked while you were growing up because they worked outside the home, you wouldn't have learned about managing people under you. You might wonder, "What kind of work did my father do when he was a basic employee? How did he change his style of working and lead his subordinates when he became a manager? I wonder if he took his subordinates out for drinks together. I wonder how he worked." You may wonder these things, but you can't try to emulate him, because you never watched him work, and so you don't know what to do. This is the first time you are being confronted by this situation. If your parents are alive, you could ask them for advice. But what if they died when you were young? Some people have lost their mother or father while they were still children or when they were still young adults.

Some sons and daughters complain that their fathers are unreliable, even if their fathers are still alive. But even if you feel this way, there must be some turning points in life when you would want to ask your father for advice. When you get a new job, when you want to change careers, when you're thinking about getting married, when you want to move to a new house, when you have a child, or when you want to send your child to a good school, it's better to have someone to go to than not to have anyone at all.

Even if your parents might give you bad advice, it's still nice to get advice from them about unknown things you have never experienced. Some parents always give the wrong advice, but you can get good results by doing the opposite of what they advise. Some parents really are like that—their advice will always be completely wrong. Even in these cases, it's still good to be able to go to them. If you are almost certain that going to your father will get you the wrong advice, you could think to yourself, "My father, who led the life of a defeated person, will have the wrong judgments. So, the opposite of what he says should definitely lead me to success."

If your mother died early on in your life, even if you've grown into a beautiful and intelligent lady with many male admirers, after you're 20 years old, it may be very hard to know how you should be and carry yourself. If your mother were alive, you would still be able to get some kind of advice, no matter what kind of mother she might have been. Being all alone, you may feel tremendous pressure and not know what you should do. The same holds true regarding the career aspect of your life.

In this way, there are times when you're given a promotion, your environment is changing in a positive way, or you seem to be moving forward in your life, but you find yourself falling into depression. In most cases, this comes from your fear of facing uncertain and unknown experiences. This is what is causing your depression.

Success and Worry Are
Opposite Sides of the Same Coin

So, in truth, these circumstances are like a coin with two sides: on one hand, they bring praise, success, applause, congratulations, and people telling you, "That's so wonderful," but on the other hand, they also make you feel anxious, worried, and insecure and bring you much unbearable suffering and many sleepless nights. These circumstances are like the sharp and blunt edges of a Japanese sword, the sharp side and the back side of the blade. Actually, you cannot gain success or receive praise without going through risks of this kind.

For example, if you had to give an hour-long lecture to a thousand people this Sunday, you might feel such incredible pressure that you feel like your hair is going to fall out. If you were just an audience member, you could happily sit and listen to the lecture, but if you had to give the lecture yourself, you would feel incredible pressure. People around you might say to you, "It's a great opportunity for you," but then you would feel even more pressure.

To add to that, a religious leader is always expected to give good lectures, so it would be a disaster if you couldn't. This would also be a very tough situation. A batting average of 0.3 or 0.4 in professional baseball is an acceptable success rate, but a professional lecturer is not allowed a success rate of 30 percent. Before each lecture, your team of staff managing the event will feel extreme pressure and will worry whether you'll be successful if you're only able to do well three out of ten times, meaning you'll fail seven times. If the lecture fails, they will face an avalanche of criticism from the audience. They will lose sleep at night, worrying about whether your mind will blank out and you'll freeze in the middle of your speech. For this reason, it takes a lot for a professional lecturer to succeed.

A Sense of Inferiority Overcomes Students Starting at Prestigious Universities

In these ways, many situations in life will seem praiseworthy and worthy of congratulations to another, objective person, while to you they feel terrifying, anxiety-causing, and depressing. To onlookers, it seems absurd to feel depressed about these situations, so they can't easily understand why you're feeling depressed. But it's only natural that you do.

For example, college admissions can make students feel anxious. When you worry about what you'll do if you won't get accepted, you start to feel so anxious that you lose sleep at night. But then, even after you get accepted, you'll still face difficulties.

It could be a junior high school, high school, or college that you are applying to, but the better or more exceptional your school, the more exceptional the student body will also be. With other exceptional students surrounding you, you will suddenly feel like just an ordinary person or even among the lowest-ranking students, like a deep-sea creature living on the ocean floor, even though, just yesterday, you were an excellent student. It's a terrible shock. You might be asked, then, why you chose to go to that school. Your reason was that you heard many people say that it's a very good school and that it would be incredible to get admitted. And then, no sooner did you enter the school than you all of a sudden became an average or below-average student or even ranked at or near the very bottom. To avoid this painful situation, you could choose not to attend this school, but you want other people to respect you, after all. So you decide to go and are then defeated in the competition.

About half or more of the students will probably be defeated, develop an inferiority complex, and get depressed. In such a case, you end up suffering from depression, even though you were admitted to the school of your choice. There are many people who have this kind of experience.

There are many famous universities in Japan. Let's say that you are attending a prestigious university such as the University of Tokyo. When you take the Inokashira Line from the Shibuya train station and get off at the second stop, at the Komaba-Todai-Mae station, a huge crowd of people will be getting off at that station with you. The majority will be students going to your university, and as you see that, you may suddenly be seized by an inferiority complex. You may not be able to help it—a sense of inferiority may simply fill you all over. When the University of Tokyo admitted you, you received a lot of praise from your hometown friends and family, saying, "Good job. Well done. Nice work." In most places, they'd regard you as one out of a hundred people and you'd be respected by others. In some areas of Japan, you'd be one out of ten thousand people. But now, you are attending the University of Tokyo, and every morning during rush hour, like a swarm of black ants, hundreds and thousands of students burst out of the trains. Seeing this, some people feel a sense of lower self-worth fill them. This is called value deprivation. This is the feeling of your self-worth being taken away, as if your self-value has been stripped from you. You used to feel important and extraordinary, but now, all of a sudden, you've become ordinary.

It's natural to feel this way. If you were a Miss Universe contestant, you'd feel beautiful standing among a group of everyday women. But standing in a crowd of 20 other Miss Universe contestants and comparing yourself to them, you might see that someone else has longer legs, is taller, has bigger eyes, or has more shapely eyebrows. Noticing these things, you might suddenly feel overcome with a sense of low self-worth. This type of situation, when you've done something deserving praise but you end up feeling shocked inside, happens very often in this world.

3

The Meaning of Competition in Societies

Without Competition, Societies Are Bound to Decline

The modern age is competitive. As long as this is the case, there will be victories and defeats, victorious ones and defeated ones. Some of the depressed feelings that modern people suffer from come from not being able to endure these feelings of defeat.

But if we got rid of competition and allowed everyone to be equal, what would happen? This might seem to be a good idea, because that way, we would never have to feel stressed, so we would never feel depressed. This is one possible view, it's true. It would create a pastoral, primitive world. No one would fall into depression from stress. But then, on the other hand, there would be decline, stagnation, boredom, and corruption of the soul. Such things would appear instead.

So, in the end, it's a tough choice between these two things: depression or decline. You might believe that your depression comes from being defeated in societal competition. But you could take another view and decide that getting depressed is better than getting corrupted. If you lived on an island all by yourself the way Robinson Crusoe did, you wouldn't have any competition, but it would be a very lonely world. Because such a world would feel lonely, human beings create societies. And when we create societies, we develop competition. In the end, there will be some people who take leadership and others who don't; some people who are competent at work and others who aren't; some people who are good at creating a profit and some who aren't; some who are good at speaking and some who are not-so-good at speaking. Competition develops in this way, and competition creates suffering. But human beings still desire to live together. It's human nature to feel this way. And as long as we feel this way, we create order in human society. This gives rise to people who feel unhappy about that and feel depressed. But even if this is the case, I feel that this is still better than eternal decline. This is one point.

Victory and Defeat Can Be Measured in Many Ways

Another point is to ask yourself, "Does the idea of the survival of the fittest determine your victory or defeat in the true meaning of the words?" There is indeed victory or defeat when we look at one aspect of ourselves only. There are wins and defeats when you look at one criterion only. It's true. For example, say one hundred people joined your company at the same time. If you look only at the timing of your and your colleagues' promotions to section manager, department manager, or an executive position, you will find that some people were victorious and some were defeated.

But a slightly different view appears when you also compare other aspects of your lives, aside from just the speed of your promotions, such as family circumstances. If you want to get promoted faster than all your peers, you might suffer if you don't. But if you were lucky and your company hired you without a fully qualifying resume, then you might expect that you'd never be promoted. In that case, you'd feel very successful if you ended up being promoted at an average pace or at the same pace as your peers.

In this way, success means something slightly different to each person. Even if someone seems successful to you as you look on from the outside, there will always be aspects of that person's life that you're not seeing. If you look at just one criterion, one aspect, one tick mark on the yardstick, then there are victories and defeats, it's true. But, in reality, we have many different yardsticks. In truth, it's not easy to recognize which people are happiest overall when those many yardsticks are combined. So, after all is said and done, it is indeed correct to say that you are happy if you feel happy. If you, yourself, feel happy, then you are. There's no room for anyone to deny it, even if other people wouldn't expect you to be happy.

If you tend to demand a lot from yourself and you're unhappy if you don't receive the highest level of respect from others, then in your eyes, this world must be filled with the seeds of unhappiness—

so much so that we might feel sorry for you. You might believe you'll get a lot of respect by being exceptionally intelligent, but in truth, people with higher levels of intelligence have stronger feelings of inferiority. They're not able to forgive themselves for small mistakes or failures. So, when they see people who are better than they are, they suffer a lot inside themselves, even if it's just one or two people.

In this way, some people suffer when just one or two people are superior to them, while other people are happy as long as they're not the lowest-ranking person. So, it's difficult to know the correct yardsticks to use to measure their happiness or unhappiness.

Religion Is Society's Antidote to Stress

Because this world is now so competitive, it is apt to produce more and more people every year who are clinically depressed or are at risk of such a condition. In such a world, religion serves an antidotal role in some ways. Religion teaches to believe in a different world from this world of earthly criteria and competitions. If you believe that this world is everything, you may feel that you're inside a living hell or an inescapable pit. But if you believe this earthly world isn't everything, then this world's victories and defeats will seem no more important than the victories and defeats of a wrestling match. You will recognize a variety of things outside the wrestling ring.

Religion often creates these things outside the wrestling ring.

Religion teaches that outside the wrestling ring, there is another, different world where people each have a very different form of happiness. There are also different ways to measure importance than the ways it's measured inside the wrestling ring. There are even different passions to devote yourself to. In this sense, religion plays a huge role in this highly stressful world.

Some people are too hard on themselves and become stressed and fall into depression even when they deserve praise. On the other hand, some people actually experience objective defeat, and others make some kind of mistake that leads them into depression. Most people who handle commodity prices and products, for example, get ulcers in their stomachs or small intestines. This is because people in a world of chasing numbers and constantly watching for gained or lost money can hardly enjoy lasting success. Some people are living on the edge in this way and just getting by, just by having some successes.

In this sense, not being in special circumstances or not having an important position is, itself, more conducive to happiness for most people. But since we don't quite realize that fact, we create our own suffering. When people feel bored, they let boredom become their suffering. When they are busy, they let their busyness become their suffering. When they get a promotion, they let their promotion become their suffering. And if they make slow progress in getting promotions, they let this also become their suffering. Even if they become rich, they let their wealth become some form of suffering. When they can't find someone to marry, or they marry a spouse who is too perfect or the wrong person, those things become their suffering, also. They suffer from not being able to have a child, from the child being too perfect, or from the child being very imperfect.

In this world, the seeds of suffering are endless. There is any number of them. But can we get rid of all of the seeds of human suffering? No, it's simply not possible to do so.

If We Didn't Feel Both Happiness and Unhappiness, We Wouldn't Know How Accomplishment Feels

The feeling of happiness or unhappiness, pain or pleasure, is relative to yourself. Without experiencing this relativity, we aren't able to feel a sense of accomplishment or success or a sense of having made progress in something. This is the reason we were created to feel both extremes. If we could only feel one of them—if, in other words, we produced only pleasure hormones or only had nerves to sense pleasure stimuli but not those of pain, cold, or heat— this, itself, would make it difficult to get through this life. Your life would be difficult if you felt happy whenever you touched the wall, pressed an elevator button, felt sunshine on your skin, felt raindrops falling onto you, or anything else.

I don't think that anyone has ever gone through their life in such a way, but if anyone is ever born only with pleasure-sensing nerves or only pleasure hormones, then this person would also be unhappy, in some sense. Getting rained on feels cold to people, usually. But it would feel very nice to this person. If there were such a person—someone who feels happy whether the weather is sunny, windy, or anything else, that person would be a rare, one-in-a-hundred-million existence. He or she would probably get locked up like a zoo animal, be put on television, and become an exhibit. Then, this person might finally feel unhappy.

In this way, we wouldn't necessarily be happy if everything gave us pleasure. Because we're able to feel both the good and the bad relative to each other, as necessary, we are able to polish our souls throughout our lives.

If you feel depressed and extremely negative about yourself, please remember this: Many people are in very positive or praiseworthy situations from an outside point of view, but are lamenting they're suffering from unhappy circumstances. Please check to see if you've become like them. Or remind yourself of the following. If you measure yourself based on one criterion, you might fall among the defeated, speaking objectively. This might be true. But, at the same time, when other, different criteria are used to measure people, some victorious ones might find themselves among the defeated and vice versa. You might be among the defeated when it comes to getting promoted, but at home, your family life might be ideal, harmonious, and abundant. People who've won the race to promotion might be winners of the criterion of promotion, but the family lives of many of them are in terrible condition. As the cost of being promoted and succeeding, they haven't had time to be at home because they were always working late. When you consider all these things and ask yourself which person you'd rather be, it may be difficult to make a choice.

4

Living in Competition against Yourself, Not Others

Your Ability May Be Limited, But Your Potential for Growth Is Infinite

In the past, I often used to say that human growth is limitless, that the world of human growth is infinite. But I've started to say, recently, that we human beings have specific capacities, that there are limits to our abilities. Because of this, you may be wondering whether my thinking has changed. What I have been trying to say is the following. When we think about human growth, we see that perhaps some people grow at a rate that goes straight upward near a 90-degree angle. But these people are very rare. There are also people who develop extremely rapidly, at about a 60-degree angle of growth. Others develop at a 45-degree or a 30-degree angle. There are also people growing at a pace of 10 degrees, 5 degrees, and 1 degree, and some are ever so close to 0 degrees. There are even people who develop at a negative angle.

But compared with the babies that we all were at the start of our lives, each one of us has basically developed in an upwards incline. It's just that the degree of everyone's development has been different for each person. The greater your angle of growth is, the faster your growth will seem compared to others. But at the same time, your angle of growth is much steeper, making your growth challenging for you, so you could find yourself out of breath. Very quick growth must resemble the degree of pressure and exhaustion of running a marathon at very high speed or running a 100-meter sprint.

What would happen if you lined up and assigned the same challenge, work, or topic of study to people with 60-degree, 45-degree, and 30-degree paces of development, all at the same starting line at the same time? It could be in mathematics or in English. The person at a 60-degree angle would make smooth progress. The person at a 45-degree angle would be a little slower, and the person at the 30-degree angle would be even slower. If you looked only at these things, you could clearly guess who is superior to the others.

If you look at each person individually, the 60-degree angle of development represents that person's ability, talent, and capacity. Each person's angle of development indicates that person's own limit, capacity, and degree of talent. So there's a limit to the 60-degree angle of development, a limit to the 45-degree angle of development, a limit to the 30-degree angle, and a limit to the 15-degree angle. If everyone began at the same starting point, which is point zero, and continued along their own angle at the same speed, they would arrive at different destinations.

But the key point I want to make is that it doesn't end there in reality. If you are the person with the 60-degree angle and you maintain that angle for life, that's a fine accomplishment. But, like the hare in "The Tortoise and the Hare," you might rest along the way. You could fall ill, face a setback, or die. There could be difficulties at home, or trouble at your company. Various mistakes could happen that would keep you from continually progressing at the same angle.

You could be exceptional, have gone to a good school, and be working for a good company, but your company might go under. There are many cases like that these days. With the rate of progress you were originally making, you might have climbed high on the ladder of success. But there is nothing you can do then. It doesn't matter how quick your promotion to department manager might have been. If your company goes under, it would be the end of that.

On the other hand, what if you work for a smaller company, one-tenth the size of the company in the previous example, but it survives and you're able to make three or four decades of constant progress at a 30-degree angle? Even though you're progressing at half the rate of the previous example, your success would be greater than the person who was progressing faster but whose company went under. This is what happens sometimes. Therefore, the differences in people's angles of development indicate the differences in their ability and their limits, but if they continue on ahead, each person's possibilities for growth become limitless.

This is why there is a limit to your ability but, at the same time, there is no limit. Your ability is infinite and finite, finite and infinite. We can't deny there are limits to our ability, this is the truth. There are different angles to our development. We aren't all the same.

However, we can't be sure whether we each will have the same angle forever, because we will go through times when we become less capable. For this reason, look at your life as a whole in this way, and tell yourself, "My life is my life. My angle of development might be just five degrees, but if I forge ahead continually and untiringly, I can have enough of my own form of happiness." Because when our angle is overly steep, we are apt to stumble and fall down due to excessive pride, and we will get ruined that way.

If your angle of development is too steep, it's essential to adjust your speed of growth. Especially if you possess innate ability, slowing down is important so you won't succeed too much, too soon. Find creative strategies to continue over a long course of time. Don't let yourself burn out completely. Adjust your speed of progress so you won't completely burn out. This is also essential to do.

For these reasons, I would like you to know that my teaching that says, "There are limits to your capacity and capability" and my teaching that says, "There is no limit to your growth" can be combined, even if they seem to contradict each other.

Long-Lasting Continual Efforts
Will Take You Far Distances

When people start something new, a great many give up within about three days. There are milestones of three days, three months, three years, and three decades that you could aim for. Keep going for three days, and if you do, then aim to keep going for three months. If you're able to continue for three months, then aim for three years. If you can continue for three years, you'll start to gain some degree of capability and skill in what you're doing. You'll start to see a clear difference between yourself and other people who have never done what you're doing. This difference won't develop much in three days or three months, but it should certainly start to appear after three years. After that, if you have lasted for three years, then try to keep going for thirty years.

With three decades of continuous efforts on the same path, before you realize it, you will have traveled an extremely great distance, even if it were at the pace of a tortoise. Usually, it's very difficult to continue for thirty years. If you continue steadily for thirty years, you will be surprised at the destination you will reach.

People with steeper growth angles might have risen up the ranks but then fallen down. Therefore, if you can keep going over a long time, aiming to reach three days, then three months, then three years, then thirty years, and if you diligently and continually go forward in this way, you'll get very far.

So, in actuality, if it's your goal to keep moving forward over a long period, it is better to have an angle that's not too steep. When you succeed very quickly, in many cases it's difficult to sustain that success. Often, your success might never return because it is so fragile. So, in many cases, not having a steep angle of development will let you keep going for a long time.

It's often said by people who adopt this strategy that the way to succeed is to be lucky, slow and steady, and tough and persistent. To succeed, you will need luck, but you will also need to be "dense, unaffected by things, and thick-headed." And then, you also need persistence, patience, and strong resolution.

Since the idea of luck is about the end result, there's not much I can say about it. But I understand when people say that dense people succeed in advancing their positions. Dense people are able to keep on going for a long time. People who are denser, who aren't affected by things and are not sharp like a sharpened knife, are able to continue for a long time. So is the kind of people who have persistence, patience, and strong resolve. So, when you look at the formula for a successful life, being unaffected by things, dense, thickheaded, and also having persistence and strong resolve are great strengths.

Genius Is Never Born without Obsessive Efforts

In addition to that, we are apt to think that talent is determined by whether we are intelligent. But this is not actually true. Nowadays, many good schools are mass-producing a large number of highly educated graduates who did well in school. But when it comes to the number of geniuses, there are many, many fewer of them. If I were asked whether geniuses are more intelligent than those who did well in school, I would say that I don't completely think so. Most geniuses did not necessarily do the best in school. There is usually a curious aspect to geniuses, something that seems to be missing in them.

The words *obsession* and *attachment* have negative religious connotations, but what I want to say is that, among smart people, becoming a genius is difficult to do without a burning desire inside you and without continually working on something for a very long time. You need to completely devote yourself to your work and think that it's something you absolutely need to do. To be able to do that, you can't be someone who is too smart.

People who are too smart get distracted by other things, try to get involved in various other things, and strive to be a jack of all trades. This prevents them from achieving great success. But someone who feels a little less intelligent than others, who knows it's not possible to succeed at everything, and who concentrates very deeply on one thing will sometimes get ahead of the group of highly intelligent people. This person will begin to shine with the light of a genius in that field.

Did this person have exceptional talent? No, that's not the case. Was this person extremely intelligent? No, that's not the case either. Of course, it wouldn't be possible to be a genius without intelligence. You need a certain degree of intelligence. But aside from that, it's essential to have persistence, a burning desire, and an obsessive will. No one has ever become a genius without those things.

I'm not the only person who has mentioned these qualities. Hideki Yukawa has also written about that. If people in Japan were asked, "Who is a genius in Japan?" most people, back then, would have said, "That would be Hideki Yukawa, the Nobel laureate." That is how well-known he was as a genius. I feel somewhat suspicious about whether some recent Japanese Nobel laureates are geniuses. But maybe it's because I've grown older now, so they don't look that outstanding to me.

Back then, in Japan, everyone knew that Hideki Yukawa was a genius. Hideki Yukawa himself said that genius is created by obsession. Because of its religious meaning, *obsession* isn't a word I'd like to use, but that's the word he used. He said that you cannot become a genius without an obsessive will to spend years and decades pursuing the answer to one question. According to him, unless you are able to strongly obsess and obsess about one question in search of the answer, you won't become a genius. People who are distracted by other things or who look halfheartedly for an efficient answer aren't able to become geniuses. In some sense, he is saying that you have to be unintelligent. You'll only be able to constantly obsess about something if you're unintelligent. This is what Hideki Yukawa said.

Since he was someone who deserved to be studied as a genius, what he wrote about being a genius must be true. There is indeed a type of geniuses, like Leonardo da Vinci, who spreads out their talent across many areas. But very few of them have appeared in human history. By contrast, many geniuses have appeared among people who dug into a narrow area very deeply, for a very long time.

There is a limitation to one's talent, in this sense. If you don't have an exceptional level of ability, you can't become a first-rate person in a field without working as many as thirty years in it. You cannot let yourself be distracted. The person who pushes ahead on the path, no matter what happens, will become a first-rate figure. It's only natural that this is true.

If you have played chess professionally for thirty years, there will be an evident difference between you and an amateur. Or, even if your foreign language grades during junior high school were poor, if you spend thirty years using that foreign language professionally, you will surely become capable in it. Thirty years as a foreign language teacher will make you a professional in that language. In this way, your language capability will grow considerably compared to others.

In this way, success can take a variety of forms for the variety of people in this world. So don't try to do everything. Don't try to do this thing and do that thing. There is a form of success that will come from your special ability, your talent. When you keep going forward in this way, you will succeed in a way that others would not be able to imitate.

In our current educational system, students are given a nationwide standardized test, the National Center Test for

University Admissions, and everyone is given a rank, from first place to last. But it's important to know that this ranking does not determine the outcome of your life.

Focusing on One Area
Will Bear Greater Fruit

To succeed in your life, it's essential to concentrate on one field deeply. Sometimes, people who are brimming with ability will succeed in two or three areas, but when they try to add too many additional areas, their ability declines in each of them. I, myself, have been concentrating on the field of religion. It's not because I am not capable of doing other things. It's because if I do a variety of things, my talent in each area gets spread out; my talent gets small when it's divided up that way. For that reason, I avoid doing too many unnecessary things and try my best to concentrate deeply on my main work. Otherwise, my talent won't bear fruit.

In some sense, being stoic with yourself means recognizing that you can't do everything and abandoning things you shouldn't do. This is essential to do. You may be surprised to find that this will bear great fruit, while trying to do a variety of things will not.

Some people who were intelligent in their younger days or who were once full of ability don't seem to have much success in their forties. I can't help but think what a mystery it is to see this happening, and I can't help wondering why they haven't been successful. I think it is because they didn't dig enough, all the way, in the field that is most suited to their true talent, and they were buried in the crowd.

In this world, there are a lot of yardsticks by which to measure your abilities, but becoming moderately good at everything according to them is not what you should strive for. Concentrating on one or another field and cultivating it in this way is essential. To do so, you will need a burning desire and strong resolve. You won't be able to succeed if you cannot keep pushing forward in that way.

You might remember many capable and outstanding classmates in high school, but maybe they gradually disappeared. As I mentioned earlier, they might have gone to a good college, such as the University of Tokyo, and as a part of the student body there, they lost confidence, their spirits shrank, and they turned into just part of the masses. This does happen. Many people also thought that a company that everyone else wanted to work for would be good to work in. But you might not know what happened to them afterward.

In cases like this, those who are likely to succeed are those who actually seem to have a bad personality. When I say "bad personality," I mean the people who don't break their own mold, who keep going ahead in their mold. They say to themselves, "This is who I am. This is my style, my thinking, my character." This type of person gets criticized a lot, but it seems that the people who don't break their mold, even when they are criticized again and again, are those who are most apt to succeed—those who never get completely knocked down and who seem to have a slightly warped side to them. In Japan, when we are trained, we are thoroughly educated not to have areas that stick out—to be well-balanced people. Some people were educated like that but didn't become that way, so their teachers, family, and peers eventually gave up on them, and these are the people who are apt to succeed a lot in their lives. This might come as a surprise. But in the end, these types of people are competing against themselves, not against others.

Enjoy the Continually Changing Being That You Are

So, in these times of depression, if you are saying to yourself, "I'm a good-for-nothing," I would like to ask you, "Is that really true? Is it true that you have become worse since you were a baby?" That isn't truly the case at all. Actually, you are much more outstanding now, overall. You are bigger and stronger. You now have knowledge, discernment, and experience. You have much richer human relationships than you did as a baby. As a baby, you didn't have money, but now you do. You might have enough money to rent a house, a condominium, or an apartment under your own name. In these ways, you're a very different person now, compared with the person you were as a baby, but also when you were in kindergarten, elementary school, and even junior high school. When you compare yourself to who you used to be in this way, you will see how you've progressed.

Because your angle is different from other people's, things won't go the same way for you as for them. But you've still made progress in many ways, compared with how you were before. For example, at 20 years old, you were probably at the peak of your exam-studying ability. This ability gradually begins to decline when you're around 30 years old. As you grow older, your memory and ability to train through repetitive practice gradually decline, after all. And when you gain more and more new knowledge, your older knowledge gradually fades. Physically, your strength also drops.

But on the other hand, you gain more experience as you grow older. And when you accumulate experience, you often find yourself instantly solving problems that used to take you several months, because now you already know the answer.

If you look just at this one point, you will see that your intelligence has grown by several hundredfolds, or even several thousandfolds. This growth comes from the power of experience. So, as you grow older, your knowledge accumulates, and you will, of course, start to forget things. Of course, your physical stamina will slowly decline. But your experience will accumulate. When you reach a certain age, other people will not be capable of surpassing your level of experience. There will be something about you that other people cannot defeat.

In this way, we have a variety of things to look forward to in our lives. When one aspect of us declines, another side of us grows. When we age, our physiological energy does indeed drop. For example, when I see beautiful singers or actresses on television, I feel nothing. It's so surprising, but I don't find them sexy or anything like that at all. It might be because I'm much older than them. But people younger than me probably find a twenty-year-old singer very beautiful and charming. Probably just the sight of her moves them so much that they want to shout from their lungs or tears fall from their eyes. In my case, though, even when I'm watching people like her perform, I don't find them so appealing.

When I see young singers around the age of junior high school children singing together in large girls' groups, they're just schoolchildren in my eyes. In a sense, I, myself, feel that I must have lost an ability. People talk about how beautiful they are. But they're just children dressed up in skirts to me. That's the only way they appear to my eyes. To people near the same age as them they must appear differently. This must be a form of joy in some sense but also a form of suffering in another sense. I can see what the true nature of the female singers must be at first glance. But other teenagers probably don't realize what I see, and the singers must appear like goddesses to them.

Over the course of our human lives, some things fade away. But new things get awakened, and we see things differently than we did before. We are living beings who are continually changing as we go through this life. Who we were yesterday, who we are today, and who we will be tomorrow are all different. This continual change is something we should be happy for. If you only look at what you will lose, it will seem sad, but there will always be something else that you gain. You're constantly changing into something else. It's important to enjoy this continually changing being that you are.

As I said earlier, some people feel so much pressure before their wedding that they break down and abandon it. My advice to them is, "Tell yourself it's all right if you end up having a second marriage. Thanks to the practice you get in your first marriage, you might do better the second time around. Or you might do better the third time around." When they hear this, they'll feel much better and they won't resort to leaving their wedding.

Also, there are people who are suffering the pressure of filling their section manager positions. Such people should hear the story about a large trading company's section manager who failed when trading speculative rubber in the market. He got demoted to an ordinary employee, but later on, he rose to the head position of that company.

Such cases indeed occur. If you continually get promoted, your life can become unbalanced. There is a side of our lives that cultivates us as people through occasional demotions. Through experiencing both ups and downs in our lives, we're able to see various things.

5

Make the Effort to Praise Yourself

Discover Your Good Points

It's a happy thing to be praised by others. In Happy Science, we teach that we should praise others correctly. We say that we should offer kind words and give love to other people. But in reality, there still are not enough people who say kind words and give love to others. So if no one seems to be praising you, then please praise yourself once in a while. Because, as I have explained just now, there are many ways of looking at yourself and you, yourself, have the greatest amount of knowledge about yourself. So, please think about changing how you look at yourself.

If you keep thinking to yourself, "I'm not as good as that person. I'm a failure if I can't be this way," then you might believe that you are a good-for-nothing person. So, look at yourself in a different way. You are now far more developed than you were in elementary school. When you were a teenager, maybe you worried that you might never get married. And now you are distressed about having a bad wife. If you look back at yourself when you were young, you'll recognize the progress you've made since then. You got married. It's a great accomplishment. You can praise yourself, saying, "I deserve praise for supporting my wife, despite how terrible she's been."

If you're troubled by having terrible children, you could look at that and think to yourself, "I deserve praise for my efforts bringing up my children, even though they've been terrible." If you're 60 years old and still working in a rank-and-file position, you should praise yourself, saying, "I must have a lot of passion in my heart to be working in this way, even though I'm 60 and still in a rank-and-file position." It's definitely possible to look at yourself in this way. You can also look at yourself and think, "It's an accomplishment in itself, that I haven't let myself get ill." If your hair is thinning, then tell yourself, "I still have a ring of hair left; I'm not completely bald. But it doesn't matter, I still have hair left." If you have graying hair, then tell yourself how beautiful your silver-gray hair looks. These are other ways you can look at yourself. So when there is hardly anyone to praise you, you should give yourself praise sometimes.

It might be unseemly to praise yourself too much in front of other people. I don't recommend putting another person down and praising yourself in front of others, the way some people might do. Sometimes, you might end up doing so unavoidably, out of self-defense. But people would not like you if you were to behave that way constantly.

So, it's not necessary to praise yourself when other people are around. It's enough to do it when you're by yourself. You might overdo it by doing it every day. But it's good to do it once a week. You can tell yourself, "Well, look, I've been going through a depression. I should at least try praising myself maybe once a week." And then say to yourself, "There must be *something* good about me, even if it's something small." At the very least, if you compare your current self to a past version of yourself, you'll definitely see that you've grown in some way. There is no way that everything about you has gotten worse. There is absolutely something about you that progressed.

If you've been promoted to section manager and are feeling depressed, feeling unconfident about fulfilling that position, think back on your entry-level years, before you'd even thought about this kind of responsibility: you're more aware of things now than you were back then. If you're feeling depressed because the pressure feels unbearable, this is a sign of your awareness of not having that much ability in you. This, itself, is an accomplishment. Many freshman employees believe that they can become the president of the company. So, if you're worried that you're not good enough to be a section manager, this, itself, shows how more advanced your level of awareness is compared to theirs. You absolutely should praise yourself for that, even if it's just a little bit.

You need to give yourself a tailwind by telling yourself, "Keep going! Fight it out! I'm doing a good job! Well done. There are good things about me, too." Please feel that way about yourself, and praise yourself. If no one will praise you, you have to praise yourself a little bit. Of course, you shouldn't get overly proud of yourself, but you need to praise yourself a little bit to lift your spirits. It's very important to do so.

If you are too depressed to do self-reflection, try to find something good about yourself to praise. But when you do, letting other people hear you could end up backfiring. If you say out loud, "I'm doing great. I'm doing a good job," someone else around you might criticize you, saying, "That's ridiculous, don't be absurd," and then you would fall deeper into your depression. So it's better to do this when you're alone and no one else is around to hear you.

Give yourself praise when you're alone in your room, and smile. If nothing to praise comes to mind, you could write it down on a piece of paper. Try to write down splendid things about yourself, or things that aren't outstanding yet but that have had progress compared to a long time ago. Right now, you might be saying to yourself, "There is nothing worthy about me. There is nothing good about me." But that's not true at all.

In Animals' Eyes,
You Are Like a Huge Supercomputer

My children have had pet rabbits. The rabbit we have now is our second one. It's very cute, gets fed, and gets to be pet a lot and taken care of, so it seems to have a very happy life.

But unlike humans, it's unable to speak a single word. It's regrettable, indeed. So, you might be saying, "I'm a miserable person. I'm not good at anything." But you're able to speak those words, and that, itself, is an incredible thing, after all. You have the language capability to express your misery in words. Regrettably, rabbits can't speak even these things.

Rabbits also don't know how to do math. They seem to understand the concept of "one," "three or four," and "many." Just these three categories. If you set their feeding times to the morning and evening but not the middle of the day, they won't come out of their cages when you go to them at lunchtime. They understand that when they are fed the first time, they won't get fed the next time, but they will get fed again after that. So they understand there is an order of being fed and not being fed. They have this level of intelligence.

Our first rabbit was able to understand some human words, such as "food" and "carrot." It responded immediately to those words when we said them. It would also win our affection by licking our hand. But the second rabbit wasn't able to learn the words "carrot" and "food" or the skill of licking our hands like the first one did. Because our second rabbit grew up in a pet shop, it never got to learn these skills from its mother. There is a difference in their abilities.

In these respects, the second one might be inferior to the first one. But, actually, the second one also has skills that the first one didn't have. To express joy, it leaps and twists its body in the air, like a fish. The first rabbit had this ability for a time, but it stopped doing that after a while. But the second rabbit has kept this ability continually. It can also act very cute and charming, rolling onto its back and showing us its belly. So, some of its abilities were better than the first rabbit's.

So, the abilities between even the same species of rabbits vary. In this sense, the principle of the survival of the fittest might be true even among rabbits. But we still see that they're only able to get hay, food, and water. They're not able to speak words or count numbers. Even if you think that you're worthless, from an animal's perspective, you are like a huge supercomputer.

Aim for a State of Thinking Nothing and a State That's Egoless

I happened to give an example about animals. But such things hold true to humans in many ways. If no one is giving you praise, then you should praise yourself. Please strive to do so. It's especially important in a depression-prone society. If you've developed a strong negative self-image, please balance that with a positive self-image. Doing so is also recommended by medical professionals. When clinically depressed patients are treated by doctors, they are advised to look at the full-scale version of themselves, to look at yourself as you are. If you are thinking too negatively, then they will tell you to think positively about yourself, to look at the full-scale version of yourself now. They encourage you to restore your self-image to the full-scale version of who you are, in light of society. In this sense, it's essential to praise yourself a little bit.

In addition to that, if you're someone who is always thinking negatively, please sometimes come to the *shojas* (large temples) or local temples of Happy Science to practice clearing out the thoughts from your mind, to practice thinking of nothing. Negative thoughts are going around in your mind constantly. So, you should practice thinking nothing.

You might not last more than five minutes. It may be surprisingly difficult to empty your mind. So it may help to start by listening to sounds of a rippling stream, a breeze, birds chirping, a waterfall, soft music, or meditation music. This will help you to stop thinking about unnecessary things and concentrate your mind. This is also very important to do.

So, praise yourself sometimes. Then, please also aim for the state of thinking nothing or a state of mind that's egoless. Stop negative thoughts from coming up, and feel deep peace in your mind. When you do, you will start to see how you, a person with Buddha-nature, should be, and also the path you are meant to walk. You will be able to evaluate yourself objectively. I hope you will give these suggestions a try.

CHAPTER TWO

.·.✲.·.

What It Means
to Succeed

Success Principles We Don't Learn in School

1

The Foundations of My Success Since Childhood

The Essential, Foundational Bases for Succeeding

This chapter is on the theme "What it means to succeed." Instead of giving a difficult discussion, I will make this discussion as easy to understand as possible, so it can become an introduction that newcomers to the Truths can get advice from.

On several occasions, I have said that success requires capital. Capital ordinarily refers to the necessary funds for starting a new business. But I don't mean capital of the financial kind only. I also mean the driving force, or the foundation, for you to succeed. I believe this to be essential indeed.

I hesitate a little to talk about myself. But because it could help my readers to have examples, I would like to look back on myself now. I've almost lived for 50 years now (at the time of the lecture). I feel that I've had great success overall in the larger scheme of things, even if I suffered at the different key turning points of my life. I feel I've been fortunate to have been born under a very lucky star.

When I ask myself what the origin of my success has been, I, of course, see that various spiritual factors have played a part. There was my soul's mission and also the support I received from Heaven. But since those aren't factors we can do so much about, I will put them aside. Instead, I'll focus on just our human lives in this earthly world and look for some kind of universal principle in them. When I look over my life in this way, I do indeed find several factors that have contributed to my success. Even when the non-earthly factors are disregarded, there are several foundations of my success that I have recognized.

Being Well-Behaved
When Your Parents Aren't Watching

One foundation of success that you can cultivate during childhood is the trust of your parents. Your parent's approval and trust are very important to your success. Somehow, I recognized the great importance of this as a child.

What makes your parents trust you? It is the way you act and behave when they aren't watching you. Children being children, they are usually well-behaved in front of people, and in front of their parents in particular. (Although, they sometimes cannot do so even though they want to.) Generally speaking, all children are apt to be this way. But there is something incredible about the parent-child relationship. Parents can somehow tell how their children are behaving, even when they're not watching them. Parents can recognize small signs and slightest things about their children. So, how you act when they're not supervising you is important. If you're misbehaving, being lazy, or neglecting things you've been asked to do, you will be found out at some point.

I was the type of child that worked especially hard when my parents weren't watching me. I'm not sure how my parents saw or sensed that side of me, but they praised me for it very often. So, it's important to behave correctly even when you're not with your parents. It's nothing special to behave well when your parents are nearby. If you cannot, it may mean that you're being clumsy or trying to be rebellious. This is why my parents praised me a lot for the efforts I made when I was away from them.

A Self-Disciplining Mindset

It was the same with my schoolwork. My parents didn't have to scold me, give me instructions, or create goals for me when my grades weren't good. I, myself, told myself to do better and pushed myself harder voluntarily. Children's usual pattern is to study a lot near their exam and play when they're finished. Of course, some children will also play instead of study even before their exams because of the stress they feel. They feel such pressure that they read novels, watch television, or do something else instead of studying.

But many children generally study a lot near their exams and play as soon as it's finished.

In my case, I was the type who studied immediately after the exam again if I thought that it didn't go so well. I would give myself even more material to study, and I would assign myself harder work if I felt I hadn't done well. My parents seemed to see this and notice that I had an extraordinary side to me.

In my mind, I had clear standards that I wanted to meet, so I worked harder and disciplined myself when I didn't meet them. Maybe it was different from a rational mentality. Maybe this was an old-fashioned ethos, a mental attitude, that goes back as far as the Edo or Meiji periods. But this kind of inner tendency was something my parents acknowledged in me.

A Non-Wasteful Attitude toward Money

My parents also noticed how I thought about money. When I received an allowance or gifts of money from my parents and relatives, my parents would watch how I used them. They watched carefully to see whether I'd spend the money quickly or on unnecessary things.

Essentially, my approach to money was to save it carefully in my piggy bank and never go to it if it was not essential or urgently needed. Only when something important came up would I use it, and then very wisely. Seeing this side of me, my parents said that I would become a very successful businessman. They mentioned this during my late elementary school years. So, this was a tendency of mine even then.

Indeed, this tendency hasn't changed much even in my adulthood. I don't spend money on unnecessary things, and I still never touch money I've gained unexpectedly. I save that money, and in fact I often forget that it's even there. It doesn't matter to me how much it is; I just never think of using money that's come to me in that way.

I never spent money on unnecessary, consumable things. If I ever spent money on something, I would use it only on things of good investment value with high returns in the future. I've been this same way ever since childhood, and I'm still like this even now, as an adult. So, tendencies like this can appear from a surprisingly early time in our lives. My parents took careful note of this side of me.

Keeping Time Precisely and Feeling a Sense of Duty toward Others

Another foundational basis of your success in childhood is your punctuality at school and elsewhere. My schoolteachers noticed that I always kept time very precisely and was never careless about time. I was always prepared a little beforehand when something was scheduled to begin. My time management was always precise in this way, so I never needed to rush myself or be in a hurry. I was trusted for being punctual, never being late, and keeping time correctly in this way.

My schoolteachers also noticed the same trait I mentioned earlier: that I worked hard even when adults weren't watching me. Teachers, too, care about how students behave when they're not being watched. My teachers seemed assured that when they weren't there, I'd be looking after things and taking care of everyone. My tendency to behave well and never let things get out of control, especially when our teachers weren't watching us, seemed to earn my teachers' and friends' trust.

I remember that when I was in ninth grade, a Japanese class teacher who taught another grade got transferred to another school in a neighboring town. I had never been this teacher's student, whether in my homeroom or in any other class, but one day, through someone else, I was told that this teacher was asking to see me on Saturday. In those days, telephone communications were not so developed, so I only heard about this request through another teacher at my school. Why did this teacher want to see me? It was because this teacher was trying to show the student council how to publish the school newspaper but couldn't instruct them well. Since I was the one publishing the school newspaper at this teacher's previous school, the teacher wanted my help instructing the students. Although it was only the next town over, it was about eight kilometers (about five miles) from where I lived, which was quite a long way, so I had to go there by bicycle. I asked other members of my school newspaper club to join me, but they refused, saying it was too far to go by bicycle. Only one person agreed to come with me.

Even then, I felt a sense of duty to go if someone needed my help. So I went to this teacher's school to help the students. This teacher had assured them that I would definitely come if I were asked for my help, because I was that type of person. So the teacher and students were eagerly waiting for me by their window. When I arrived, everyone clapped for me, saying, "You really came!"

There was a side of me that felt a strong sense of duty. I felt a responsibility to keep my promises and fulfill my duties to other people. I didn't want the feeling of owing something to someone.

Test Grades Cannot Measure the Essence of Your Life Perspective

Everywhere, in both the East and the West, it's said that ability is essential to success. But looking back on my life, many people with greater ability than me in various areas did not necessarily become successful. Many of them didn't succeed much at all, and many others have completely disappeared, to be frank.

Why is this the case? In terms of school grades, they were exceptional students. But a basic difference between them and me was our life principles and how much other people trusted and relied on us. As people, we have qualities that our school tests cannot measure. For example, there are qualities such as cheerfulness, positive and constructive thinking, and how well we reflect on our mistakes, keep promises, and behave ourselves while no one else is watching. It was these kinds of qualities, the ones that test scores don't measure, that made a difference. When I look only at this-worldly reasons for my success and put aside the spiritual ones, I see that the huge gap between rival students and me must have developed from our different life principles.

Your life principles can't be seen in your exam scores. They are the very essence of your life perspective. As you live by them in various life situations, the difference between you and others will gradually appear. They were the basic reason that such a great difference between me and many exceptional students appeared later on. Some not-so exceptional students have still achieved relative success because their life principles follow the principles of success well.

Learn the Principles of Success
That Schools Cannot Teach You

To become successful, you have to do as much as you can to learn the principles of success that schools don't teach. It's very difficult to teach people about them. For example, schools cannot teach you how to make a profit or how to become rich. To be able to teach these things, the teachers themselves would need to have grown rich. But most teachers in elementary schools, junior high schools, high schools, and universities are not wealthy. Some might have become wealthy by inheriting money from their parents. But if the teachers themselves were intent on making money, they wouldn't have become teachers or scholars. So, generally speaking, teachers and professors are mostly not the types who become rich. This is why schools aren't able to teach their students how to become wealthy people.

How to choose a good boyfriend, a good girlfriend, or a good spouse to live happily is another subject you don't learn in school. This is also quite a difficult subject to teach. Some parents might be capable of teaching it. But since many parents have made mistakes in marriage, they might not know what to do either and so don't know what to teach their children. Because of this, children often simply follow their parents' ways and make the same mistakes their parents made.

Along the same lines, schools also don't teach how to make human relationships go well or coordinate them well. Schools and cram schools can teach how to improve exam scores and pass tests, but they can't teach how to make a lot of money, find a good spouse, maintain good relationships with friends and acquaintances and further develop those relationships. There aren't any schools that can teach those sorts of things.

For this reason, the truly important lessons in life exist mostly outside the boxing ring. As we live outside this boxing ring with no one to teach us, we all learn by what we sense from our experiences and the people around us. The only people who learn these lessons are those who manage to learn them on their own.

2

The Right Mental Attitude toward Financial Wealth

Examine Your Actions from the Public's Point of View

I've said that being trustworthy is an important foundation of success. Earning others' trust takes a lot of time. Trust can be ruined easily, but it requires time to build. It's built from how you as a person tend to think in certain situations.

When I was younger and basically still a freshman in my job, someone once said that if I ever hailed a taxicab to take me from the Tokyo train station to Nagoya City, the driver would probably take me there. When I heard this, I wondered whether I seemed that trustworthy, even to a taxi driver. Tokyo and Nagoya being very far apart (about 160 mi), the driver would wonder whether you were being serious and would want to make sure that you'd pay the fee. It's that far of a place to get to. But my colleagues said a taxi would take me there.

I realized that this is how others saw me. It's true that I always felt a sense of responsibility to do what's right regarding money. And to my surprise, this side of me appeared also in my atmosphere.

When I thought about this, I realized that this indeed was true about me. Once, when I was a student and went out for dinner, I was given 50 yen (about 50 cents) extra change. When I got home and realized what had happened, I walked 500 meters back to the restaurant so I could return it to them. They were surprised to see someone do that in this day and age.

If I had pocketed that change, going back to the restaurant would've made me feel uneasy. Since their staff might remember it and notice that I had come back, I would have felt uncomfortable to go there again. So that I could keep comfortably coming to this restaurant, I went back to return the change even though it was a small amount. To my surprise, people sensed this quality of mine even in a different situation.

When people lose others' trust, it's often due to money-related issues. So, actually, it's very important to avoid mistakes or being messy when you are lending money, borrowing money, or dealing with money-related matters of any kind. Some people work very aggressively at their job but are surprisingly careless in this area, and they would make mistakes with small sums of money.

When you are principled, you carry an atmosphere of having a proper attitude toward money, and that atmosphere naturally repels people who tempt others into wrongful profiting. People seeking to ensnare or deceive you will stop coming near you naturally. For example, if someone said to you, "By keeping dual accounts, you can embezzle taxes and use that money to buy a racehorse. Will you work with us?" you would never agree to do so. So, because they'd fear that you'd expose them, they wouldn't approach you with such offers in the first place.

Some government officials will embezzle taxes and use the money to purchase artwork. But it's such a trifling amount of money, to be frank. If you're aspiring to advance in your career, you absolutely should never do such a thing. But people give in to these small temptations anyway. They create secret funds and pocket the money, or they misappropriate it somewhere.

If you want to achieve great things, however, it's regrettable to let such a mistake destroy people's trust in you. As they say, "The day has eyes; the night has ears," so, sooner or later, everything will be found out. It's impossible to deceive everyone forever. If using money dishonestly is a bad tendency of yours, it's important to nip this in the bud.

Knowing that these different eyes are watching you leads to the spiritual aspect of life, after all. At Happy Science, I've taught that our guardian spirits, guiding spirits, and Heaven's high spirits are watching over us. This is something people thinking about committing wrongful deeds don't want to hear. It's because they think that no one is watching them that they're capable of such things. That's why they don't want to listen to such teachings or believe in them.

When this belief of being watched by invisible beings of another world takes another shape in terms of the material world, you become aware of the public eye. It means that you will look at yourself based on this viewpoint.

If you see yourself from the viewpoint of the public eye or your guardian spirit, you won't misappropriate or embezzle public funds even if no one around you is watching. For example, if you took some cash register change for your lunch while looking after the store, thinking no one would ever notice that you did, doing so could ruin your entire life. Some bank workers also pocket money from the bank for small things, and by doing so, they ruin their lives. Considering the consequences, it's ridiculous to do such things. But some people make such mistakes, believing that no one is watching them.

For this reason, it's essential to believe that invisible beings or your own conscience are watching over you. You have to want to be self-disciplined and tell yourself, "Since there are great things I want to achieve in the future, I shouldn't let such a small thing ruin my reputation." Basically, people who can't be trusted to be alone with money won't advance in their careers.

Income You Haven't Worked For Could Ruin Your Life

Many religions are very negative about money. In Christianity, people who believe in old-fashioned Christian teachings deny money automatically, believing wealthy people have difficulty entering Heaven. Early Buddhism viewed money similarly, and there is a story that goes like this: Shakyamuni Buddha and his disciples were on a mountain path when they came across money on the ground. When Shakyamuni Buddha saw it, he said, "There is a poisonous snake," and his disciples agreed, saying, "Yes, it's truly a poisonous snake." They then continued on their way on this path. But someone who happened to be listening to them wondered why they thought so, and pocketed this money. Later on, this person was accused as a criminal for doing so.

Stories like this are told often in religions to warn people against money. This story's moral is that money gained illegally—meaning, through robbery, embezzlement, or fraud—will ruin your life. It's a universal principle that's as true today as it was 2,500 years ago. Religions teach you to fear money because desiring it could sometimes lead people to illegal deeds and their future could be destroyed.

Apart from gaining money illegally, another way money could ruin your life is getting income you haven't worked for— for example, by inheriting money from your parents. Being principled when inheriting wealth is something very few people can do. Income you haven't worked for is one kind of easy money, and some people squander it quickly. They increase their standard of living and spend extravagantly. But afterward, they can't bring their standard of living back down, and they face their own ruin in this way.

In this sense, life insurance might seem useful, but acquiring tens or hundreds of millions of yen (hundreds of thousands or millions of dollars) due to someone's death is frightening. In case something happens to you, leaving your family with emergency funds from life insurance is good. Your family would be thankful for it if you ever got into an emergency, like a traffic accident. But there is something frightening about the idea of receiving money due to someone's death. Murders are committed to collect that kind of money. In the world, people are getting money in this way.

People also ruin their lives by winning 100 million yen (one million dollars) in the lottery. They can't avoid the people who flock to them. As they keep treating people to things, things gradually start to go wrong. They become unable to work diligently. Or the news of their lottery money creates a commotion, so they can no longer work well at their jobs.

For this reason, income you haven't worked for can often lead to your ruin. Some people feel lucky to suddenly acquire illegal or unearned money, but it's something to be very careful about.

Accumulating Honestly Earned Wealth Is Admirable

Profits from land prices jumping tenfold, your apartment's value shooting up, your golf membership's value rising, or your stock values increasing tenfold or a hundredfold are other ways of getting unearned money. Although these kinds of life experiences are fine once in a while, becoming accustomed to them could lead to your destruction. It would be only a matter of time before this happened to you, because this wealth is only temporary and not long-lasting. A counter-effect will definitely eventually come.

It shouldn't be made a basic part of your lifestyle or the course of your life. It should only be considered incidental income, as if it doesn't even exist. If you win the lottery, don't think of it as actual income. Put it in a separate part of your accounts, and use it toward an emergency or give it away as donation. Donating some of it (planting happiness or investing towards your future happiness) and sharing it with others is a good idea, but using it for your own living expenses will lead you to your downfall. In this way, it's essential not to let money ruin your life.

On the other hand, working diligently and building your savings are admirable. It's because when you do these things, you are accumulating income through your efforts. If we don't acknowledge this meaning of capitalism, human beings will stop making efforts.

There are many ways to gain money without working for it. Besides what I have already mentioned, such as inheriting your parents' wealth, getting insurance money, and winning the lottery, there are other ways to get money, for example by getting government subsidies and preferential taxes. There are people living off government subsidies, and others receiving government business funding toward unnecessary things. If you get knee-deep into such methods, it will corrupt even your soul. It is extremely dangerous to live in that kind of way. Be careful not to live that way.

If you are currently living off of such money, it won't last for long. Instead, you should definitely choose to do honest work, to earn your income by getting compensated for the work you do. Heaven will appreciate your doing so. The mindset of getting fairly rewarded for the proper work you do is essential. Of course, it's not good to receive ten- or a hundredfold the income you actually deserve. But if your mindset is to seek fair compensation for your work, you will make few mistakes in your life, and the world around us will also improve.

If you come into a sum of illegal cash or huge wealth that you have done nothing to earn, it's essential not to react happily. As a matter of fact, be especially cautious. To keep your life from getting ruined, the respectable way to gain wealth is to accumulate it through diligent work.

Be Very Cautious of Communist Thinking and Honest Poverty

In addition to believers in traditional religions who often deny money extremely strongly, there are people with strong communist and socialist ways of thinking. They usually say things like "Making money is evil" and "Big business is evil." We need to be on guard against this type of thinking. Criticism like that is fine to some degree, and the mass media says such things probably out of some sense of duty. But if they want to deny other people's righteous efforts or the success of hardworking people, they won't succeed through their own efforts, either. This is something you have to be aware of.

If you believe that rich people, big businesses, successful entrepreneurs, or anything that gathers wealth is evil, then you, yourself, cannot become wealthy. The course of your life gets clearly determined by whether or not you adopt this way of thinking early in your life, meaning in the first half of your twenties. It's all right for you, yourself, to live a life of honest poverty. All the priests of olden times lived this way, and I believe it's good to live a pure and humble life.

But some people who think like that want to live on other people's financial support without getting their own job, as I mentioned earlier regarding people receiving subsidies. Be careful not to become this way. Some single people still receive money from their parents, even as grown-ups. They seem to be called "parasite singles" here in Japan. They live a very easy life, living with their parents, being fed by their parents, and working only when they need money but not otherwise.

Among people who believe in honest poverty, many don't want to work in the first place. This is something to be careful of. Becoming this way, in the end, will mean that you are taking something from other diligent people. Even though people of this type aren't earning enough to pay taxes, they think to themselves, "This is great. I'm lucky. If I earned more money, I'd have to pay taxes, so I'm going to work only part-time jobs to keep my income low enough." This kind of mindset definitely won't lead you to become wealthy. You should actually be thinking to yourself, "As a citizen of my country, I'm embarrassed by being unable to pay taxes. I want to earn enough to at least pay taxes to my country." Whether you're paying taxes or not, you're still allowed to use the public facilities and various benefits. You're allowed to use the roads, parks, and schools, and that is all thanks to others who are paying taxes to fund them. You shouldn't feel as though you've benefited from not paying any taxes, whether they're personal or business taxes.

Be Glad for Righteously Accumulated Wealth and Put It to Good Use

Basically, be careful with unexpected income if it's illegal or it wasn't earned through work, because it could ruin your life. But it's not wrong to use honestly accumulated income to enjoy abundance in your life. It's not wrong to acknowledge your efforts and use your hard-earned money to grow your business, improve your personal life, or do other such things. Heaven would also be glad about that kind of spending.

The course of your life depends on the feelings inside you. If your feelings deny this way of thinking, then you can only become financially poor. If you limit becoming poor to yourself, then it's fine to do. But if you let poverty become a system involving others, a great number of people will suffer. You will seek poverty for everyone equally and think of ways to seize rich people's money through taxation, resulting in many people's suffering. It's not good to live in this way.

Numerous religions view financial wealth negatively. Indeed, you can't bring money with you to the other world. But your financial wealth is the result of accumulated effort in this world. So, it's important to feel glad for the righteous wealth you earn and to use it for good uses. It's not wrongful for your businesses to grow from doing beneficial work for the world. It's not wrongful to become capable of supporting many people's livelihoods, either. Please don't let yourself overlook this point.

Misunderstanding this point will lead to ideas of spreading poverty to everyone and would only take us backward in time. Neither Shakyamuni Buddha nor Jesus Christ left sufficient teachings on this topic. But they lived in a very different time. We shouldn't apply past teachings to these modern times too straightforwardly.

In addition, it's a fact that money enables more efficient use of your time. Money lets you shorten the amount of time you spend doing various things, which lets you save a lot of time over the course of your life. It's good to look at this point positively. Even though I'm a religious leader, I thought in this way from early on in my life, and I think it was one reason I developed Happy Science so quickly. This principled attitude toward financial wealth was one factor that led to my success.

3

The Right Way to Choose Who to Marry

What Happens When You Marry for Physical Beauty, Wealth, or Educational Background

Schools also don't teach you success principles for dating and choosing a marriage partner. It's said that your IQ score isn't related to how well you do in the area of love, of being in love with someone. From what I've seen myself, I think this is true. People who are known to be extremely intelligent could do terrible things in relationships. On the other hand, people who are not necessarily highly intelligent could do consistently well in the area of love. So, how well you do in the area of love isn't related to your academic ability. In fact, if you study too much, it could dull your intuition and sensitivity and lead you to make mistakes in love.

Generally speaking, you'll develop friendships and romantic relationships, and from there, you'll choose someone as your marriage partner, your spouse. If your parents have a sound perspective on life, they could be your role models for a successful relationship. But here, I would like to give general advice to everyone, including those who don't have such parents.

Often, if you marry a partner solely for physical beauty, you end up with a broken marriage. Especially as a young person, this isn't something that can easily be helped. But it's essential to find something besides physical beauty. If you marry someone for an enduring quality in that person, you will have a lasting marriage. But if you marry only for physical attractiveness, your marriage will be short-lived. There is any number of younger and more beautiful men and women, so just pursuing beauty would be endless. Of course, you wouldn't be marrying someone if you didn't feel at all attracted to that person's outer appearance. But it's not good to make that your highest priority, because if you do, your partner's beauty will disappoint you five or ten years down the road. It could be an arranged marriage or a love marriage, but either way, if you marry based only on outer appearance, you can expect your marriage to fall apart over the course of three to five years, or ten years at the most.

This means that finding your partner's enduring quality is important, not just good looks. What could this enduring quality be? Basically, it is the person's basic perspective on life. This is the first quality you have to recognize. There are human qualities such as honesty, sincerity, frankness, and integrity. If you are drawn to qualities like these in the other person, your relationship shouldn't do badly.

Sometimes, people will look at whether someone is wealthy or not. About 80 percent of women are drawn to rich men. Often, a man who's not so good-looking will get married to a very beautiful woman if he's wealthy. In all frankness, it's clear that these marriages are for the money, and there is a lot of risk to these marriages, because it's a difficult kind of marriage to find lifelong happiness in. It's sometimes possible to do so, but if you're the woman, a marriage crisis will come when your beauty fades, and that time definitely will come.

People will look at educational background as another factor of marriage. It's said that only 50 percent of highly educated people become successful in their work, meaning, 50 percent won't succeed. So, half the time, marriages based only on educational background will fail. Since highly educated people have attended schools and cram schools with other highly educated people, they also want to work where such people gather. But, although they might be happy there, there's no mistake that getting a promotion there will be difficult. At a company where about 10 percent are highly educated, they'd have an easier time getting promoted to executive positions. But at a place with mostly highly educated people, they may never get promoted beyond the level of a basic employee.

So please know that marrying based just on outer criteria, such as educational background, will lead to later regret. Your spouse will seem very attractive when you are marrying. When you tell others about your spouse's prestigious university, like the University of Tokyo for example, or their employment at a prestigious, well-admired company where it's 20 times harder to get hired than at other companies, everyone will applaud you, saying how lucky you are. But your spouse could get defeated in the competition and not even manage to become a section manager. He or she may end up remaining a basic employee.

You're required to recognize this aspect of your spouse. But it would be difficult to recognize it if you're only chasing potential wealth. Whether a person will be tough enough to win in a competitive environment is difficult for you to foresee. Seeing someone's resume, you might think they'd be a good spouse for you. But you need to consider various things beyond the resume and predict whether a person will survive the competition. If you fail to do so, you might find yourself in a difficult situation 10 years down the road and being pitied by others. So, a high level of education is a general factor of success, but you should know that sometimes, it doesn't lead to success.

People Who Use Status and Income as Bait Don't Have Inner Substance

Other than being highly educated, status is another sought-after factor. People are drawn to high status. For example, there are people who marry doctors, lawyers, judges, and government officials for their status or qualifications. But you should look carefully at these people's interests, the areas they're cultivating themselves in, and what they are doing on their days off. There are so many people who you could marry for their status, but who don't have substance as people. They are a dime a dozen. Maybe the people who get drawn to people of this type don't have much inner substance themselves. But many people who are vocal about their status do, indeed, lack inner substance.

In contrast, as you engage in your hobbies, interests, areas you're cultivating yourself in, community activities, and volunteer activities on your days off, you may meet people and develop relationships with them without knowing their status. Only later will you find out that they have high status. People you meet in this way are generally those who become successful.

The type of people who immediately say, "I'm a doctor, you know. Doctors with their own practices don't make less than 30 million yen (300 thousand dollars) a year," are practically tricksters, craving one woman and then the next. They always approach other love interests in the same way, trying to trick them. People who mention their status or income as soon as they meet you are generally of that type.

Being attracted to that type of person means there's also a fault in you, so you can't completely complain if you're tricked and abandoned later on. But generally, there's no doubt that people who lure you with their status or income from the outset don't have much substance as human beings.

People with inner substance don't mention such things when they first meet you. Usually, they don't like being recognized by those things, so they hide them, and instead, they want people to recognize the good aspects of them as human beings. They don't want someone who finds them attractive because of their wealth. It's people who think, "I'm a high earner, but I don't want someone who loves me only for my money" who will earn wealth continuously.

On the other hand, people who use their money to attract someone will spend all of it quickly. Usually, this is people with easy money. Once you get married to each other, you'll use it up together and that will be the end of it.

So, people on the road to success don't talk about their educational background, status, or income. They don't think of using such things to attract someone. If someone is trying to attract you with such things and seems to have everything, you usually wouldn't be wrong to think that something's not right about that person's background. Those who succeed through true capability wouldn't ever speak about such things in the beginning, even if they had them. The people who succeed are the type that gradually reveals their true character when their character is acknowledged, for example, when they hear someone say, "Your way of thinking resonates with me," "You have a wonderful hobby," "You are a very cultivated person," "You have such a wealth of artistic sensibility," or "I find you so easy to talk to."

To be able to find a partner like that, you'll need to be wise. Unless you're wise, it's difficult to discern that kind of person. People who aren't wise need to be careful, because they'll act too quickly based on outer appearance or the first page of their date's resume.

So, men who will become wealthy aren't seeking women who see them only for their money. It's important to know this. None of them like that kind of woman. They like women who see them not for their wealth, but for their character as a person, their sense of integrity, their efforts, or their capabilities as human beings. If you are attracted by these things, you will be seen as someone who understands him and he will want you as his life partner, but not if you are someone who sees him only for his money.

Marry Someone Whose Character Attracts You

In addition to the men who use their money to lure women, many men marry women for their money. In Japan, this typically happens when the woman has a dowry. For example, men with big future ambitions, such as becoming a politician, usually think about taking advantage of women's dowries. Many government bureaucrats are that way. They're introduced to many women seeking an arranged marriage, and many choose someone for her dowry or her father's connections. Sometimes these marriages can be successful, so I will not criticize them that much. These types of couples are like two peas in a pod, in the end, so there isn't much I can say about that. They should get married if they are attracted to each other that way.

But a truly first-rate person wouldn't marry a woman for her father's vacation home in Hayama, yacht, dowry of 50 million yen (about 500 thousand dollars), or promises to build them a house.

Frankly speaking, this is not a first-rate person. A man of first-rate material dislikes such things. He doesn't want to take advantage of someone else's success to succeed. If your significant other happens to come from a family with properties, houses, cottages, or yachts, I think that's fine. But you can't expect much from a man who seeks those things from the outset. However well-educated he is or however high his status is, a man marrying you for your yacht or a vacation home in Karuizawa is not much of a person. Such things could be bought in any amount by working and earning his own money. So, if he's seeking such things from early in his life and thinking of enjoying himself, he won't turn out to be much of a person.

Some women from a family with wealth and high-status might also use these advantages to attract men. At get-togethers or during dates, they may boast about their family wealth and property, huge dowry, or fathers' support if the man runs for elected office. But they are not the women you should marry if they mention these things from the outset. They're not the type of women to seek as your wife. If your true aim is to become successful, they are not the type you want to marry. Unfortunately, men and women of this type are just artificial lures; no real bait is attached to them. They're using artificial bait to lure people to them.

The men and women who dislike artificial bait are the real things. Those who jump at artificial bait might be reacting honestly, but they will have little depth to them. Jumping at such bait is like using money you won from the lottery, insurance money, or inherited wealth toward your business. That wouldn't make you much of a person. If you are an aspiring entrepreneur and are starting a business using money you've earned and saved, that's very admirable. However, if you do so with hundreds of millions of yen (millions of dollars) you got from selling property you inherited from your deceased parents, be aware that businesses like this generally fail.

It's the same with choosing who to marry. If you decide to marry a woman within an hour of meeting her because her father is a major bank's executive director, it means that you're not much of a person. To fall for such things in the very beginning, both people must be at fault, indeed. But nothing good can come from these situations, so, actually, you have to hate these situations. At some level, it's necessary to be a good match for each other, so, in an arranged marriage, it might be necessary to look at various kinds of information, such as personal histories and occupational backgrounds. But it's better to marry someone whose character you find attractive. That way, you won't make a mistake. You should be careful in this point.

In the world, there is a mysterious paradox. When you chase what you desire, you do not get it, but when you're not chasing it, it comes to you. If your desire is to be wealthy, marrying a hardworking, tirelessly working person whom others trust will lead you there, in time. You have to see into his character if you are the woman. If you are the man, it's sad to marry only for physical beauty and family wealth if you don't think she's very intelligent.

Success Comes to Those Who Are Highly Self-Disciplined

For doctors, money is required to open a private practice, so there are many medical students seeking to marry rich women. What happens to this type of person after marrying? After he opens his practice, he will have an affair. Since he married just for the money, it's only natural for him to do so, once he acquires his goal. This is how doctors' affairs begin. This is what usually happens.

A similar situation occurs with businessmen who get promotions. Usually, when a man around age 40 becomes a section manager or a department manager, or when he builds a new house, that's when he begins an affair. Having achieved one of his life goals, he now feels accomplished. He wishes that others would praise him. But after 10 or 20 years of married life, his wife is too busy to praise him and feels worn down. Deep down, she feels it's only natural he'd get promoted to section manager after so many years or it's natural that he'd build a new house after 20 years. For this reason, she doesn't praise him.

Deep down, he feels very proud of becoming a section manager, of having several subordinates under him, and of getting this position a little more quickly than many of his colleagues who started at the same time. He feels like a king now. But because his wife won't praise him when he really wants it, he winds up in an affair with someone out of spite.

The woman he's having an affair with compliments him, saying, "You got a promotion! You're a department manager now. How incredible!" Then he spends money on her, saying, "You're lucky, you know. Not many people can go out with someone like me." But as soon as his money runs out, the relationship usually ends, too.

Because men are proud creatures, they want to be praised. When a man wants praise and isn't receiving it, he will find someone who will treat him like a wealthy man, even if he doesn't think much of her as a person. If he's not wealthy enough to have a mistress, he can go to a hostess bar or a high-class restaurant to enjoy himself.

To the most exceptional men, however, it doesn't matter whether they get promoted or their income increases; they will always keep working honestly. This is the type of man you can trust. It's good to be careful about this point.

Being human beings, some people let themselves go too much when they receive undeserved recognition. This is why you must go back to the starting point from time to time and remember the spirit of diligence and self-help. In some sense, letting yourself go too much comes from having low aspirations. Your having been working at a large corporation for 20 or 30 years and having now become a section manager shouldn't matter in this sense. It's not an event to boast about much. It's true that many others are still at the basic employee level. But your advancement is not much to boast about.

To our amazement, people who truly succeed become even humbler the higher their position gets. People who become humbler when rising to a section manager position will eventually rise to a department manager position. And people who are humble when rising to the position of a department manager will eventually rise to an executive position. When they get this position, they think, "I'm not at all fit for this position yet. With my current level of learning and capability, this promotion could be one or two years too early. I should make harder efforts." People who think this way and make efforts earnestly are the type who advance another level. But those who believe they deserved that position five years ago will usually be let go within five years' time. In this way, people who are too easy on themselves don't last. You cannot last if you are not the type that becomes even harder on yourself as your position rises.

Being human beings, people tend to find quick routes to success appealing. What's truly essential, however, is to always be thinking of a way to keep succeeding over 10, 20, and 30 years, to continue succeeding until the close of your life.

4

Making Human Relationships Go Smoothly

Being Overly Proud and Picking at Others' Flaws Ruffles Human Relationships

Besides these issues about money and the opposite sex that I've talked about, you must think about human relationships in general.

Making human relationships go smoothly can be very difficult, indeed. All different types of people in the world can become your superiors, subordinates, or colleagues, regardless of their true ability, and that means that troubles with them can sometimes arise. We can fumble in our relationships with them. Indeed, we can't completely avoid these situations.

How can we get out of these situations? How can we mend our relationships when they get strained or uncomfortable? In this kind of situation, it's often the case that you have become too proud of yourself and puffed up. Thinking that you're better than others, you tend to look at their weak points and pick at their flaws. Capable people become that way easily. People who get ahead of others more quickly notice others' flaws very keenly because of their better understanding of what it takes to succeed. It's the reason they get ahead more quickly.

So to them, people who don't know how to succeed seem clumsy and dull-minded. Capable people see others' flaws so clearly that they want to point them out. In this way, being smart and being capable of seeing people's flaws and weak points easily are closely related traits.

They can see their own shortcomings but also those of others. It's good to be more stern with yourself in such cases. But, if instead, you become more severe on others while being easy on yourself, your relationships will usually get ruffled and won't go smoothly.

Humbly Keep Polishing Yourself as a Person and Cultivate a Generous Heart

When things stop going smoothly in your relationships, you must go back to the starting point, go back to having an innocent mind, and reflect on yourself sternly. It's also important to end your habit of picking at people's flaws. Of course, there are differences in people's level of ability. Some people are capable, and others are not so capable. But the value of a person isn't determined just by his or her capability. There is a broader variety of human facets. Human beings are multifaceted beings with various sides to them, including personality, the ability to act, physical stamina, human character, accumulated experiences, and other things. It's impossible to see all these sides of someone and measure the person completely. This is something that's essential to know.

Usually, you're measuring someone one-sidedly. You're measuring just one facet and labeling the person as good-for-nothing. It's essential to stop your habit of picking at people's flaws. Instead, you're required to see if you can find good points in them. When you do—and this is indeed incredible—even though you don't say to them, "I'm sorry I spoke so harshly to you that time," or "I've been looking only at your bad points all this time. I'm sorry for being that way," they will sense these thoughts in you. This happens just by changing your mindset and way of thinking. Then they will also start reflecting on themselves. They will start thinking, "It was bad of me to dislike and speak ill of you so much." When you change your way of thinking, it connects to the other person and makes them change their way of thinking.

In this way, you'll realize that you've been making a fuss about small things. When you start stumbling in a human relationship, stop picking at the person's flaws, acknowledge the person's strong points, and wish to give him or her praise. If you're unable to do so in person, say your praises in your heart. Then, that person will begin doing the same thing at around the same time. Indeed, it's incredible that you'll coincide with each other in this way. Please try this. What I say will definitely come true. You can try this with your superior, your colleague, or your subordinate. If you have feelings that say, "He is really inexcusable," "I really dislike her," or if you're always thinking ill of someone, put those thoughts aside, and instead, please think the opposite things. Think about the person's good points.

When you speak badly of others, it's usually a hidden way of boasting about your own capability. You're trying to tell others how capable you are in a hidden way. This is the reason for your conflict, so, put that habit aside, and instead, cultivate a more tolerant heart so you notice more of the person's good points.

To keep succeeding over the course of a long life, it's essential to desire to discipline yourself, to a degree. For a time, you can win and succeed in different ways, but to succeed in the long term, you need to want to discipline yourself and keep polishing yourself humbly. Then, since being self-disciplined is also apt to make you severe with others, you need to cultivate tolerance and generosity.

For example, some politicians have a high level of ability but can't seem to succeed. This is because their high level of ability makes them harsh with others, and because of this, people don't want to support them. The same thing sometimes happens with CEOs.

As the opposite of that, Takamori Saigo (1827-1877) is known to have drawn people to him like a *mochi*, a sticky rice cake. Everyone who came near him would adore him. This kind of character is another kind of human ability, an aspect in we human beings that we also need.

Patience, a generous heart, and forgivingness are great strengths. They definitely cannot be measured on a test. They're strengths that bring people together, like *mochi* at New Year's sticking together, and they gain you more supporters. If you are too harsh with others, you'll only see them leave your side. It's essential to have a degree of generous heart that accepts other people.

This is a kind of human ability that lies outside the "boxing ring." At one point or another, a setback will come to you if you try to succeed using only your ability. Don't think only rationally; think also outside of rationality. We human beings possess something outside of rationality. We also have feelings. In this sense, it's a great strength to have patience, forbearance, to be accepting, to turn a blind eye to people's mistakes, and to let people's harsh words go by.

There is not just one path to success, but a limitless number of paths. It's not just one path that leads from one mountain ridge to another. There are a variety of ways to succeed. There are many sides to human capabilities, so it's important to develop various capabilities in yourself and to progress little by little.

Being Independent Creates True Friendships

In conclusion, I would like to add one more thing. Usually, people seek to create smooth human relationships to gain others' consolation and help, both in the financial sense and concerning their work. People usually seek such things.

But actually, it's important to do the opposite of that and do things on your own, without needing others' help. It's important to do things by yourself as much as possible. This is called being independent. It's easier to be friends with someone who strives to be independent, who doesn't rely on others' support, whether financially, work-wise, or at home. When two people of this type come together, they can easily be friends and help each other.

In contrast, a long-term friendship is difficult to develop with someone who requires emotional and financial help and gets many people involved. It's like a relationship between creditor and debtor. When just one side needs help constantly, a true friendship can't flourish.

If you're seeking true friendships with others, don't try to become overly bonded with them. Instead, do the opposite: take care of yourself on your own a little more. Be self-reliant, and be a little more independent. Try not to let others take care of you, and try to take care of yourself. It will make it relatively easy to develop relationships with you.

It's a mistake to think that always needing the help of others means that you have deep relationships and many friends. This isn't truly a friendship. Self-reliant people of a truly independent spirit are those who can really come together respectfully, as equal friends, as in the saying, "Great people meet as water meets water." I don't think anyone would want to be friends with someone with a debt of five hundred million yen (five million dollars). Would you want to? You'd be afraid that he or she might ask you to become a cosigner. It's quite difficult to be friends with someone whose business is in a slump and who's knee-deep in debt or whose various family troubles are erupting. It's indeed a wonder but happy people become even happier and unhappy people become even unhappier.

If you're wishing for help from others, first please cultivate a spirit of self-help and try to help yourself. Become independent financially, mentally, work-wise, and academically, as much as you can. Make efforts to be self-reliant and stand up on your own two feet. The more you do this, the more easily you'll form ties with other people. Those ties will develop into relationships, and those relationships will lead to larger personal and professional networks.

I'll tell you again that no one would want to be friends with someone who's in a lot of debt, and I mean not only financial debt, but also mental debt. It's hard to become friends with someone who lacks self-reflection, has unsettled issues, and has a mountain of worries. Be careful of this paradox.

Earlier, I said that if you want to become rich, you shouldn't depend on someone else's wealth. It's the same in human relationships. If you seek friendships, become someone who can live independently. If you do so, you will make many friends. If you don't, you won't build many friendships. Please know that there are many paradoxes like this in our lives. I would be very glad if all my readers could find hints to their success in this chapter.

CHAPTER THREE

Success That Prevails from This World to the Other World

Hints for Understanding The Laws of Success

1

Success in Both This World and the Other World

In this chapter, I would like to give you hints for understanding *The Laws of Success*[1], another book of mine. It's a book I've written from beginning to end about how to become successful. As I mentioned in its preface, I was 32 years old when I originally wrote that book. At that time, only two years had passed since I started Happy Science. As I now pick up *The Laws of Success* again and see how bold my teachings were back then, I am filled with feelings of wonder and, at the same time, something profound.

At that time, my larger lectures had only just started to get on track, and I was beginning to speak to audiences of one thousand. So, I didn't have any long-term foundation of success to ground my self-confidence. But regardless of that, a strong feeling in me said, "I want to go in this direction. I want my self-realization to be in this direction."

After publishing the first, original edition of *The Laws of Success*, I republished it 16 years later as an addition to the Laws Series. I went through the entire book again at that time and checked whether what I had thought and written were correct. In the end, I couldn't find anything in particular that required revision. The teachings on success that I'd written there were already that complete.

There are a huge number of books in the world on how to succeed. But there is something we need to be careful about. It's related to this point: "There is the kind of success that's limited to this earthly world. There is also the kind of success that abandons this earthly world and focuses on the next world. But I am teaching the kind of success that prevails from this world to the other world."

Religions often say, "You'll succeed in the next world," or "You'll be happy in the other world." But since no one has verified the actual outcome enough, we want to feel some satisfaction with our earthly success and happiness, too. We can't completely ignore this point.

At the same time, I'd feel regretful as a teacher of the Truths if you were to succeed in this world but then have a completely different outcome when you shed your body and go back to the other world.

2

Seek to Develop
Yourself and Others Together

It's Difficult to Remain Successful
When People Dislike You

Among books that preach this-worldly methods of success, there are some whose teachings will lead to Hell. What kinds of teachings are these? In essence, they encourage you to focus on accomplishing your own interests and selfish desires.

By dint of the law of thoughts, our strong thoughts often become reality. So, if we look at self-realization alone, we see that people with stronger desires succeed more easily than others. This is true. In addition, if you don't mind ignoring other people, causing people trouble, or hurting other people's feelings, you can get ahead of others very quickly. If you don't let people's criticism, backbiting, and tears bother you, you can feel a shallow happiness for your subjectively great success.

It's a success method that's especially preached in sales-related books. When you're focused on producing numerical results, you can just ignore all things that obstruct you or that cause you to hesitate or be indecisive. You'll seem to succeed quickly in this way.

But, usually, such success also causes negative reactions during this earthly life, before you pass away.

Even if you're hated by people, you could be successful in this way for some time. But such success is difficult to maintain on a continual basis. This is because our happiness as human beings also comes from other people's heartfelt support and gratitude.

Ignoring other people's feelings about you and feeling self-satisfied could be one kind of "enlightenment." But as we are social animals, human beings live as a community by trait. And since we do, if you were happy while hogging all the happiness, you would resemble a monkey who is happy while hogging all the food. You would feel happy as you're eating the food. But other monkeys would criticize and be jealous of you. Some monkeys would complain that you weren't being fair.

To avoid this, you need something that justifies the tremendous quantity of the obtained food. For example, sharing some amount of it to the other monkeys might gain their approval, even if you give them less than you give yourself. Or, for instance, your success should seem well-deserved, either because it came from your hard work or you've been their leader protecting them from outside predators.

When Deciding How to Live Your Life, Think of God's Eyes Watching Over You

Living with many enemies seeming to surround you is not a happy circumstance. Such a life would be unhappy, lonely, and, in some sense, alienated. You would want to think this issue through during this life before worrying about what would happen in the afterlife. You would go through life with people's jealousy and criticism weighing on you, and you would be hated by others. You could end up becoming an old, openly egoistic person.

An even stronger word for "egoism" is "egotism," a mental attitude of worrying only about your own self-interests. People will accept a little egoism. But you will be very hated by others if you live egotistically, thinking only about yourself and not minding sacrificing others. For this reason, you have to be careful not to cross this fine line.

When you pass on from this world, your state of enlightenment—your state of mind—will determine whether you become an angel or a *bodhisattva*, or a being of Hell. For this reason, always be aware that God's or Buddha's eyes are watching over you. Keep His value judgments firmly in your mind as you think about how you will live in this world. It's a point you must not forget about.

This is the difference that clearly divides numbers-based methods of success from the Laws of Success that I teach. In other words, it is good to seek success and to succeed. But please also shine light upon others as you do. Please at least desire to do so.

Strong Self-Sacrificing Feelings Lead to Tragedy

On the other hand, there is another approach to success that says, "I don't seek any success for myself. I wish it only for other people." But when this sense of self-sacrifice becomes too strong, it can give rise to a tragic quality of letting bad situations arise. For this reason, I don't encourage feelings that say, "Let me perish, but let others flourish." You could, indeed, win people's acceptance more easily by saying, "Let me perish," "Let all suffering come to me," "Only I need to suffer, so others can have happiness." But such feelings might in fact draw those outcomes to you.

I believe each one of us should take responsibility for our own life. This is why I feel it's better to feel some fulfillment and happiness of our own, as we each live our life. A self-sacrificing approach to success is self-destructive and also impacts many other people. It's good of you to think of the benefit of the world and all people. But one self-destructive family member doesn't affect just that person, in the end. A great deal of trouble will fall on numerous people, such as parents, brothers, sisters, relatives, friends, acquaintances, and many others. They will be concerned for you, take pains for you, and deal with the aftermath for you.

For example, it's noble for a CEO to feel sad seeing ill and starving African refugees on television. But what would happen if he sold his house, all his property, and even his business and then donated all his profits? He would make himself penniless, and the life of his business would end, as a result. He would then fall ill, burdening many people around him. Because he'd need everyone else's support, he'd be placing on them the great burden of taking care of his terrible mess. If such a situation resulted from his deed, it would be a sign that he was lacking some form of wisdom.

If you're a business owner who truly wants to give continuous help to diseased and unfortunate people, you should pursue the steady, continuous growth of your business and use your profits to fund donations and volunteer services for them. You should develop this kind of system. By doing so, your life will be one of fulfillment, you won't bring misery to people around you, and, in the final outcome, you will successfully provide long-term aid to those suffering from disease and economic difficulties. Selling your house and property is not so difficult to do. However, financial resources like those can quickly dry up. It's an outcome that's as clear as day.

If you act too hastily in a great rush to succeed, overly strong feelings that say, "I hope to produce immediate results to get recognized," or "I want others to give me recognition" might lead to deeds that God or Buddha isn't truly wishing from you, even if they come from a spirit of self-sacrifice.

Share the Know-How of Your Success with Others

If I were to compare my Laws of Success to something else, I would say that Sontoku Ninomiya's (1787-1856) approach to success is similar to mine. He put selfless dedication, every ounce of his wisdom, and tireless efforts into successfully reviving villages and provincial governments' finances. He invented a new economic principle and became a founder of the spirit of Japanese capitalism.

When he was spreading this spirit of Japanese capitalism, Sontoku Ninomiya drew on his own resourceful wisdom, succeeded on his own first, and then taught others the know-how he had gained from his success. Whether it was to reform a farming town or rebuild a local government's finances, he poured all his wisdom into building a continual system of success that would last 100, and then 200 years. I believe that everyone should live as he did, if possible.

I encourage you to seek to develop yourself and others in combination. Then, because we as human beings tend to desire slightly more personal benefit, it's important to hold such a desire back and discipline yourself to wish for more happiness for others. I hope that you will think in this way.

Successful People Seek to
Be with Other Successful People

In *The Laws of Success*, I also wrote about how to join the city of successful people. It's very difficult to join the successful if you have not been successful yourself. They say that in the U.S., a town of retired people of a certain level of success and fortune doesn't admit unsuccessful people who cannot support themselves.

A fence was built to surround this town, there is a guard stationed at the gate, and people have to pass background checks to be admitted. Why are these things done? Because unsuccessful people or, put another way, people who envy successful people and want to use up others' wealth are, in some sense, takers. Because of this, the town gets ruined when they're admitted, making the successful people want to move out. Successful people seek other successful people's company in this way.

Therefore, if you seek great success, it's important to first use your present capacity to create a small success. You can do so by drawing on the funds, connections, educational assets, and talents that you have now. In addition, you should achieve these successes in a way that benefits other people and society as much as possible. And as you go on, you should further expand your success while sharing it with other people.

Often, religions' views of corporate businesses and corporate work are simplified, saying they're evil. But I don't think that this is always necessarily true. Even in corporate work, if your business' higher-level to lower-level workers have the constant desire to help and benefit others, and are thinking of helping others help each other get through difficult times, I believe that your business shines with light.

3

The Mindsets of Saving Happiness, Sharing Happiness, and Planting Happiness

It's essential to enter the path to success in this way, while always correcting your mind. In other words, it's important not to become focused just on your own self-interest. As the novelist Rohan Koda (1867-1947) described, there are three principles that are essential on the road to success: saving happiness, sharing happiness, and planting happiness.

Saving happiness means you won't become too proud of passing success. Put another way, it means that you won't use up all the wealth or profit you've suddenly gained without giving deep thought to it, and you won't run your business recklessly, without thinking about the future. It means that you will treasure and cherish this wealth instead.

Sharing happiness means you will share the benefits of your wealth with other people.

Planting happiness means you won't use up all the money, assets, and other things you might currently want to use, and instead, you'll save this money for your future or invest it for your future life, 10, 20, 30, or 50 years down the road. Although they say that you shouldn't be attached to money, it does not mean that you should be spending all of it immediately.

Planting happiness is like planting trees for forestation. You're apt to want to buy consumer goods and things of immediate use to you. But happiness planting means that you'll instead plant trees that will mature several decades from now. Then you can harvest and sell them for profit 30 to 50 years down the road. In some cases, that will not happen until your children's, grandchildren's, or great-grandchildren's generation. In that case, you will be planting for the sake of people 100 or 200 years later. In this way, happiness planting means thinking about the future and offering part of your current earnings to the future's fruits.

The principles of saving, sharing, and planting happiness are important foundations of your success. Success means you have gained a fortune of some kind. The Japanese words for *happiness* and *luck* contain the character for *fortune*. Therefore, saving happiness means using your fortune carefully, sharing happiness means sharing your fortune with others, and planting happiness means planting the seedlings of future fortune. These are essential things to do.

At Happy Science, we also value the principle of happiness planting. If you use your entire earnings on yourself, you couldn't say that you have noble aspirations. It's only natural to want to spend, for example, your 200,000 yen (about 2,000 dollars) income all on yourself. Perhaps it's even more natural to want to spend

300,000 yen (about 3,000 dollars) on yourself, even while your income is just 200,000 yen. It's not easy to donate 20,000 to 30,000 yen out of that paycheck to, for example, fund Happy Science's religious activities, the building of *shojas* (large temples), and missionary work. With that 20,000 (about 200 dollars) or 30,000 yen (about 300 dollars), you could treat yourself to something delicious, play golf, go out for drinks, or go to the karaoke bar. It's not easy to take such an amount out of your income and donate it to a religious organization.

But the donation from you and people all over the country and the world will combine, accumulating a tremendous sum of money. This money we gather can build *shojas* around the country and overseas, start new religious activities, and fund various publications.

By offering a part of your hard-earned money to activities beside your own, you are helping generate an even larger movement. These religious activities can then offer many people opportunities to get back up from a setback, become happier, and become successful. They can help stop people who are contemplating suicide and encourage them to start over in their lives. They can help people suffering from illness regain their strength. They can help people revive a declining business and move it toward success. In this way, they create a chain reaction of happiness, a virtuous cycle, letting the 20,000 yen or 30,000 yen enlarge into a tremendous power. It's a very precious practice indeed.

4

Bringing Personal Happiness and Public Happiness into Harmony

Don't Keep Your Success All to Yourself

As you start to succeed, it's crucial not to keep all of your success to yourself. I mean that it's not wrong to hope to become a section manager, a department manager, or an executive of your company. There is nothing wrong in wishing for such things. It's very painful and discouraging to work very hard but never get recognition or respect from other people. To be able to work continuously over the course of decades, I think it's helpful to pursue advancement in your career.

But on your way up to section manager, department manager, or executive positions, it's important not to concentrate all work and personal aspirations on personal success. At the very least, create a little breathing room, and don't keep everything for yourself. Don't fill your "one-liter bottle" all the way to the brim with yourself. Keep 100 milliliters or 200 milliliters empty for others to join. On your way to becoming a department manager, for example, help others succeed too. Recommend them for something, or share your know-how with them. When you share the blessings of your success with others, a great many people will come to approve of and support you.

When you're succeeding, you'll usually become the target of a lot of envy and jealousy. This indeed happens and to some extent can't be helped. Actually, if success didn't exist, human beings wouldn't have any reason to feel jealous. No one would feel jealous of someone who is unsuccessful. So, being the target of people's jealousy is indeed a sign that you are succeeding. So, you must accept that becoming a target of jealousy is to some extent unavoidable.

Then, when you do become the target of people's jealousy, it's essential to always wish to live for the sake of others. You don't need to show this outwardly, but you should always hold this feeling in your heart.

Also, when other people achieve greater success than you, you will feel these competitive and jealous feelings inside yourself, too. When you do, you must control them as much as you can and praise their success, even if it goes against your true feelings. Congratulate them on their success.

For example, if another company becomes bigger and bigger compared with your company, don't say, "They just got lucky—things just worked out for them purely by chance." Instead, it's better to be able to say, "That's incredible work by your company. I hope that our company will succeed like yours has." As the saying goes, "He who hurts another hurts himself." When you wish unhappiness and failure upon others, this small-minded heart will attract failures also to yourself, in the end. You wouldn't want to cheer on, assist, or applaud someone who was wishing for others' failure. On the contrary, you would want to support someone who was wishing for other people's happiness. It's the same thing. People will dislike your company if its success brings unhappiness to all the rest of the companies. It's good for your company to grow, but to keep succeeding, you need to want to do your best to help your whole industry and, by doing so, also bring wealth to your country and the world to the greatest possible degree. It's important to control your desires in this sense. Wishing for other people to succeed could make you seem overly nice. But if a great many people come to support you because you refrain from acting selfishly and control your desires, then your happiness and success will bear great fruits.

Human Beings Exist in Support of Each Other

Buddhism also teaches the law of cause and effect and there are two aspects to it: cause and effect over time, and cause and effect in space.

Cause and effect over time is the vertical principle of a cause leading to a result. This teaching says that a good cause yields a good result and a bad cause yields a bad result. In other words, good deeds that benefit others will eventually lead to good outcomes, and bad deeds will also eventually come back to you. This is the law of cause and effect over time. This teaching is the more famous one. But there is another side to the law of cause and effect.

It's what I call spatial cause and effect, which is a horizontal relationship. This kind of cause and effect runs through your relationships with other people and the world. It means that, we, human beings, don't go through life all alone.

It's said that the Japanese character for *person* is an image of harvested wheat straws supporting each other. This is exactly right: human beings' existence depends on us supporting one another. Whether it's husband and wife, parents and children, brothers and sisters, friends, or acquaintances, we all exist in support of each other. We cannot go through life alone. Human beings indeed exist while we support each other. When something goes smoothly for you, turning your life's cogwheel in a positive direction, your cogwheel then turns another, adjacent cogwheel. When the father succeeds at his job, his wife and children become happier, which spreads this happiness further, to others. Maybe some people don't let a single seed of happiness leave their home, but usually when one thing gets better, other things get better too.

This means that human beings exist in mutual relationships with one another. Improvements for you are also improvements for other people, your company, your society, your country, and the world. The opposite is also true. Improvements for someone else impact other people, including yourself. A company doing better leads to the company's workers also doing better. On the other hand, the workers of a company nearing bankruptcy won't reap much good no matter how hard they work. It wouldn't matter how exceptional they were, there is nothing they can do when their company goes under. In a recession in an industry, various companies collapse and get restructured. In these cases, also, the workers have no power to do anything.

Your company is also further influenced by your surrounding society and country's policies. It is additionally influenced by whether your country's principles are based on freedom, a market economy, communism, or a military dictatorship.

So as others influence you, you also influence others. You are this kind of existence. Many things exist while mutually influencing one another. It's important to be aware of this and have this perspective on the world. This is the reason that spatial cause and effect is another aspect of the law of cause and effect.

Understanding this law of cause and effect lets you see that becoming happier doesn't end with yourself. Your happiness impacts other people, and this impact occurs mutually.

It's the same with international trade. By both importing and exporting goods, two countries can "play catch" with each other, enabling them both to prosper. A country can sell its surplus goods to another country that is lacking them, and vice versa—the former country can also purchase the latter country's surplus goods.

Industrialized nations can export their manufactured products to developing nations, and developing nations in turn can export their raw materials, natural resources, and agricultural products to the industrialized nations that need them. Through this trading process, both countries become happier. This is the shape of international trading, the principle of commerce, which is indeed a part of the law of cause and effect.

In international trade it's not possible for just one side to prosper while the other side loses wealth. In a war, when one side wins, the other side gets defeated. Triumph and defeat occur clearly in a war. But it is different in the world of trade, commerce, and work. In this world, engagement can never result in one side completely winning and another side completely losing. Instead, everyone mutually helps one another.

When an automaker makes huge profits, the benefits of its success aren't limited to that company. That automaker's many subcontractors also gain a lot of work. The subcontractors will then purchase raw materials and various other necessities from many other companies. In this way, many companies are connected with one another. So, when the automaker grows, various companies are able to succeed. On the other hand, when the automaker's business fails, so will the subcontractors' businesses and other businesses that had relationships with them.

In this way, mutual relationships are at work in economics. The same is true for politics. There are horizontal relationships in these worlds.

For this reason, we can't say that we only need personal happiness or that we only need public happiness. Personal happiness and public happiness are apt to contradict and conflict with each other, but it's important to wish to bring them together in harmony.

The points I have talked about so far are the basic themes running throughout *The Laws of Success* overall. I'd be glad if you'll keep these key ways of thinking in mind as you study that book.

5

The Success of Organizations

If there is anything further I would add to *The Laws of Success*, it would be the following point. Since *The Laws of Success* focuses on individual success, some slightly different ways of thinking would be required if I were to discuss organizational success. For an organization to succeed, it needs a sense of balance, a general plan for the organization as a whole, and ways of fixing and repairing weak points, flaws, and shortcomings.

When numerous people are working together, an individual's personal aspiration is not enough. The harmony of the whole, balance, and the right kind of management are essential. I've written on this topic in another volume of the Laws Series, entitled *The Laws of Invincible Leadership*[2], so I recommend this book for useful hints on this topic. But please be aware of this point: to lead an organization, you need another view and to think from a higher standpoint.

At the same time, the theoretical teachings for an organization and an organization's leader before they start succeeding are exactly the teachings on personal success that I've given in *The Laws of Success*. You will succeed by following that book exactly.

But when the organization grows beyond a certain scale, you will need to use wisdom and think things through more and more deeply. You will need different ways of thinking to handle various matters. You should definitely keep this point in mind.

6

Determine on the Thought First

Finally, another teaching running through all of *The Laws of Success* is that your thought comes first. It's your thought that exists first, and it's then followed by various other things. It's another, basic theme running through *The Laws of Success*, so please don't disregard this point. Please cherish this teaching that says, "First there is a thought. It then becomes a reality afterward." You must determine on the thought first.

People who have the right thought but aren't successful usually have weak resolve or waver over time. You're unable to wish from the depths of your heart for the success that you don't have the capacity to achieve. Even while you're saying, "This is what I want to become," you also doubt yourself or deny it at some level. Please consider whether you can deeply wish for your dream to come true during deep meditation. And as I said in the prologue of this book, *The Laws of Hope*, you must also check to see if your wish is righteous and also right for you.

In addition, the teaching that your thought comes first also applies to the relationship between your mind and your body. You have to choose between wishing for health and wishing for illness. There indeed are people who subconsciously wish for illness.

They're the type of people I mentioned earlier, who lead self-destructive lives.

Please decide which you want to wish for from the bottom of your heart. If you wish for health, then continue hoping for it strongly. By doing so, your thoughts and state of mind will influence your body, which is like the shadow that always follows you. The many who read *The Laws of Success* will surely see their health conditions heal. Please live cheerfully, positively, constructively, and enthusiastically, just as I taught in *The Laws of Success*. And please also live with a blithe and breezy attitude.

NOTES

1   See Ryuho Okawa, *The Laws of Success* (New York: IRH Press, 2017). See page 219 for more information on this book.

2   See Ryuho Okawa, *The Laws of Invincible Leadership* (New York: IRH Press, 2018). See page 221 for more information on this book.

CHAPTER FOUR

Becoming Invincible

How Organizations' Leaders Need to Think

1

See Success or Failure as Victory or Defeat

Sometimes we use the word *invincible* at Happy Science, as I have done in the title of my books *Invincible Thinking*[1] and *The Laws of Invincible Leadership*. This chapter presents my various thoughts on the meaning of this word, *invincible*.

First, I should discuss the question, "Is there such a concept as 'victory versus defeat' in religion?" This indeed is just a matter of expression or wording. But, usually, each one of you has a certain criterion for determining your success or failure. You have some aspirational standard that means success if you reach a certain point and failure if you don't.

But instead of seeing things as just "success versus failure" or "happiness versus unhappiness" in this way, you could see things as "a victory versus a defeat." Victories are when you surpass this aspirational standard, and defeats are when you don't. You could reconsider your life from this point of view as one way of looking at things.

By seeing the problems of your own life, organizations, societies, and even nations mainly from this point of view, you can make judgments surprisingly rationally, without letting your emotions and feelings sway you. Often, thinking various things emotionally sends you into a vortex of worries. So, you should sometimes put your emotional conflicts, emotional burdens, and various other feelings aside and rationally consider your problems in terms of victory versus defeat. Try to determine what constitutes a victory and what constitutes a defeat to you. Calmly analyze yourself, the world you live in, and the circumstances surrounding your work from this point of view. When you do, sometimes you'll easily solve problems you couldn't find any way to solve before. Sometimes, looking at problems in terms of victory versus defeat lets you find the solution surprisingly clearly.

2

See from a Broad Perspective

Win Overall,
Even if You Suffer Small Defeats

Another viewpoint goes even further than that, beyond just the idea of winning versus losing. It concentrates on a way of not suffering complete defeat. When failures keep coming and the air is thick with possible defeat, focus on what you can win to avoid losing completely. This is a defense-based viewpoint—looking at what you should win to avoid complete failure. Find the area where winning will ensure that you'll avoid complete defeat even if you fail elsewhere.

Still another approach uses more positive thinking. With this approach, you think about what you need to succeed at to win overall. If you make sure you win the key point that guarantees overall victory, then you can ignore everything else at the cost of being defeated in some small battles.

Consider focusing on these two viewpoints I've just discussed. Usually, we are prone to thinking about winning at everything versus losing at everything, but that's not what usually happens in reality. So, don't think in terms of complete victory versus complete defeat. Instead, think how to achieve overall victory even at the cost of some failures. This is one viewpoint you could consider taking. So, think of what to abandon in order to succeed as a whole, and find what needs to be done to do so. Alternatively, find the one victory that will let you avoid complete defeat, even at the cost of suffering small defeats. This is another way of fighting. The point is to have a bird's eye view, an understanding of victories and defeats as seen from the general situation. This is the broad perspective I discussed in *The Laws of Invincible Leadership*.

A Broad Perspective Has to Be Cultivated

Seeing from a broad perspective is indeed very difficult. But to achieve great success in your life and be a leader of others, this viewpoint definitely needs to be cultivated in you. When subordinates come to you, their leader, to report their failures at this and that, they won't get so shaken if these failures don't seem to be an overall defeat to you from the broader perspective. Your subordinates won't get nervous if you clearly know where failure can be afforded without completely getting defeated, and if you firmly know the minimum necessary success that ensures that everything will be all right.

When you can lead others in this way, people who otherwise react nervously to each victory and each defeat will calm down.

Your subordinates panic often because they don't know if something means victory or defeat. For that reason, their emotions sway left and right with each little incident. But relief will come when they know that you can distinguish victory from defeat and that you're watching things steadily, from a broad perspective. Actually, they'll relax and will just wait to receive your judgment. If you say it's not a defeat, they'll trust that it's not a defeat. If you say it's a victory, they'll trust that it's a victory. They'll know to leave this judgment up to you, their leader, and they'll concentrate on their own work.

But often, it's difficult to see what small victories and small defeats mean from a broad perspective, so some leaders make judgments based on trifles. Under such a leader, subordinates look at small failures as total defeats, and sometimes, they'll all run away from the situation. This is the difficult part. It's similar to an army regiment that retreats at the sound of waterfowl wings flapping. Indeed, everyone has a lot of fear. People being human, they'll feel the urge to run away even at a slight hint of defeat. In times like that, your ability to see the general situation makes a big difference.

A broad perspective is indeed an ability you're sometimes born with, but it also doesn't emerge unless you develop it. It's rare to find children with a broad perspective or great insight. Perhaps once in a while, there are children with these abilities. But they would be mature beyond their years and would not be so lovable. They'd seem too cheeky and overly mature as children, and they wouldn't receive much affection from their families, friends, and teachers. In this sense, they would be on a path of defeat in life, and this would mean that they didn't have the right broad perspective. After all, it's probably better for children to succeed the way other children normally do and to mature smoothly into adults as they grow up.

So it's rare to be born with a broad perspective, but some children do indeed display surprisingly wise judgment. It's not impossible to be born with this ability, in this sense. At the same time, your broad perspective will actually develop when you're a little older. It emerges in adolescence, at first. Then, it gradually develops after age 20.

3

Succeeding with Others Under You

The First Turning Point Is at Age 30

If your path of success in life started relatively early, at a young age, your abilities tend to be easily noticeable. If your path of success started when you were young and other people see you as successful, then you are quick-thinking, very versatile, and able to seize opportunities. Without these qualities, you couldn't have become known in your teens or twenties as a capable person. These are qualities that many people can easily assess. Actually, without such qualities as shining talent and the ability to work quickly and succeed in a short span of time, you couldn't have won others' recognition.

But there are two groups among such people. The first group of people doesn't further develop their abilities. If you're a quick-thinking, versatile person and you find that you've stopped developing your ability, people's assessment of you will reverse at some point, just as you begin to have subordinates working under you. In a basic employee position, you'll be highly appreciated if you have ability and competency in your work. But around when you begin getting subordinates, the criteria for recognition change. It won't be enough anymore to succeed by yourself. You'll be required to succeed by using the people working under you.

The ability to manage people becomes essential now, but people who are capable are prone to be poor at using subordinates. Because they, themselves, are so highly capable, they think, "He's not good enough. She's not good enough, either," which makes them unable to use many of their subordinates. If you just can't feel fully satisfied unless you do the work yourself in your own way, it will be difficult to delegate work to others. You won't be able to use your subordinates to accomplish things, because you cannot delegate work to them.

On the other hand, when you, yourself, are not highly capable, you're more apt to delegate work to someone else with capability. Knowing that you're not competent, not able to work quickly, and lack versatility, you're more apt to seek out and use other people who are versatile and capable.

You can start to assess whether you have this quality around the age of 30. Your first turning point starts to appear around this time. This means that people who are capable of using subordinates can't be differentiated from people who are not until they turn at least 30. Both these types of people may already have high levels of ability themselves and are ranked against each other, but you can't tell whether this is the true ranking order until they are around 30 years old. If you are striving to be in the spotlight after this age, more often than not you're prone to drowning in your own ability.

On the other hand, around age 30, some people start to think about communicating about their work to others and getting people to work for them. They were also highly capable people up to that point, but they now restrain themselves from showing off their intelligence and ability.

To be able to do this, you need to have confirmed to yourself that you have some level of ability. You'll require some level of confidence in and foresight about your future, your level of ability, and the general level of work you're capable of. You'll need to continually try to prove your ability to yourself if you're unable to get a sense of this by around that age. You won't be recognized by others unless you keep striving to prove your capability, so you'll keep going in this way. But if around age 30 you can confirm your level of ability and the level of work you can do, so that you feel self-assured and self-satisfied, you'll stop spending 100 percent of your energy showing off and proving your ability to others. You'll put part of that aside and, instead, you'll start thinking of ways to succeed by combining your ability with other people's abilities.

Can You Take an Opposing View into Consideration?

Until this point in life comes, capable people are generally talkative. Many are quick-witted, have much to say, and reach the conclusion before their superiors finish explaining. They'll tend to respond mid-explanation, saying that they understand and will work on it immediately, without their superiors finishing.

But if you are one of them, you will start around age 30 to speak sparingly and to listen to others, including their opinions. Even when people's views sound absurd to you, you'll still listen to them a little bit, thinking, "Maybe that's another way of looking at things," "Maybe there's a kernel of truth in this person's view." You won't just stick to your own views. Instead, you will consider whether there are useful hints in the other person's viewpoint. Even if you don't take in the other person's views, you will actually value him or her to some degree for having a different or opposing view. When you were younger, you focused on debating and winning against others who gave different opinions. And whenever you won, you used to think, "I won, I won!" But you steadily develop a certain level of seasoned experience after that.

You might not see much of a difference between, on one hand, charging ahead without any awareness of the opposing viewpoint and, on the other hand, charging ahead while being aware of it but having decided your view is right. From the outside, these may appear to be the same things—but indeed they're different.

When you're aware of differing and opposing views, a special quality and depth appear in your work, even though you would have done the same thing anyway. Somehow, the surrounding people sense this about your work, so your work begins strongly impacting others more. People recognize this "light filtering through the cracks" of your work, and they can tell that you're aware of other, opposing viewpoints and of the possibility of them also succeeding. In this way, they recognize that your decisions and actions are intentional. They can see that, in that case, there must be some further, deeper thinking behind your decisions. By contrast, if you're only thinking about winning versus losing, they'll think, "Do what you want. If you fail, we'll all just laugh."

In this way, even if you don't adopt the people's own views, they will acknowledge and follow you if you're a leader with a deep understanding of their opposing views. The reason is that they foresee that you will shift direction and take in opposing views if you find that your decision was wrong. But if you see others as rivals from the outset and crush those with opposing views, you will never accept another person's opposing opinions.

What I've explained in this section is one of the capacities of a leader. Whether you develop this capacity or not will determine whether you'll grow into a leader.

Adolf Hitler Ignored Advice from His General Staff

Adolf Hitler, Nazi Germany's leader during World War II, served in the lower ranks of the army during World War I. As a noncommissioned officer in this war, he crawled around in the mud on the battlefield, dodging enemies' bullets, and survived. But while he was struggling in the mud, the General Staff Office members were discussing unrealistic strategies from a safe and clean headquarters. They were making decisions on paper and ordering the army to do this and that. It seems that this had frustrated Hitler who was a lowly corporal risking his life, never knowing when he would be shot at.

Hitler had never been a military elite. He was originally an aspiring painter who didn't get into art school. So he was not particularly gifted with strong military capabilities. But he had some ability in devising visions of the future. So this quality of an aspiring, visionary painter in him became useful later on.

When he became the central figure of World War II, he ignored the advice of his General Staff and did the opposite of all their suggestions. A side of him enjoyed showing them that doing the opposite could win them battles. Naturally, he would sometimes win, even when he didn't follow the General Staff's ideas. So, he kept refusing their suggestions and said, "Look, I was right." But always fighting internally, in this way, hinders collective power. Eventually, the group will be faced with the individual person's limitations.

So, before Hitler was defeated by external enemies, he had already been defeated internally. Many failed assassination attempts were made in his last days by his own General Staff. Being targeted by his own men in this way, he obviously wouldn't have been able to win against external enemies.

The General Staff saw Hitler as a commonplace and not very talented leader. They saw this clearly about him because he never listened to the advice of professionals at fighting war like them. Things would have been different if he chose different approaches after considering their advice and demonstrated his own talent in that way. But it was clear to them from the outset that he didn't ever intend to listen to them. Occasionally, his unconventional way of fighting the war resulted in victories. But he lost the war in the end. This was because the professionals' strategies had greater possibilities for victory in the long term. This is how Hitler was defeated.

Lessons on Succeeding with Others Working Under You in *The Records of the Three Kingdoms*

There is a similar example from the Chinese classic text, *The Records of the Three Kingdoms*. This describes the period of the Yellow Turban Rebellion, which sent the country into chaos. It was a time when rivaling warlords strove to defend their territories, many heroes emerged, and many alliances and rifts occurred as people fought for control of the country.

Among them was Yuan Shao, a warlord in North China, who held a lot of power for a time. With a large army, he fought against Cao Cao, who would later become the King of Wei. It is said that Yuan Shao had an army of 700,000 soldiers while Cao Cao had just 70,000. Being outnumbered ten to one, Cao Cao didn't seem to have any chance of winning, but he managed to win in the well-known Battle of Guandu (200 CE). Cao Cao won with an army only one-tenth the size of his opponent's, and this changed history.

During this battle, Yuan Shao's military advisor gave him various kinds of advice, but Yuan would not listen to him. When the military advisor suggested an opposing view, Yuan sent him to prison. As a result of that, Yuan returned home with an army nearly completely destroyed. So, the prison guard said to him, "It's good news. This proves that the advice you gave him was right, so he should be releasing you soon." But the advisor's response was, "So Yuan Shao lost the battle? Then I won't have much longer to live."

When Yuan Shao arrived home, the military advisor's words came true. Even though the advisor's advice was right, he was put to death anyway. This was the way Yuan Shao used the people who worked under him. When someone had a different opinion, he took it as a criticism of his mistake, and so, one after another, he put to death the people who expressed opposing opinions. He was very similar to Hitler in this respect. People like this may become powerful for some time, but they will eventually suffer defeat because they alienate people.

Compared to Yuan Shao, Cao Cao had a strong desire to gather capable people to himself. Cao Cao mustered numerous military generals. He also gathered strategists through showing his utmost respect to them. As a result, no matter how hard the Kingdom of Shu fought under their military strategist, Zhuge Liang, in the end, they could not defeat the Kingdom of Wei, whose foundation Cao Cao had built. Although it's true that the Kingdom of Wei's national strength was five times stronger than the Kingdom of Shu's, the Kingdom of Wei was still abundant with capable people anyway. This was due to Cao Cao's character as a person.

Cao Cao was a strong military general in actual battle, but he was also a capable military strategist. People of his type generally tend to dislike other capable people, but he sought them out anyway. He was capable enough to write a military strategy textbook, but he didn't shrink from seeking other capable people. As a result of that, the Kingdom of Wei was full of many capable people.

In the Kingdom of Shu, Zhuge Liang especially stands out as a military advisor. But in some sense, this shows that they lacked other capable military advisors. They also had especially well-recognized military heroes, Guan Yu and Zhang Fei. But when you consider it, the Kingdom of Wei had so many military heroes that none of them stood out as individuals. This tells us that Cao Cao was highly capable of using organized power. With numerous advisors and generals at his command, he was able to dispatch one and then another into battle, a strategy that let him fight battles indefinitely.

Cao Cao often lost individual battles, but it didn't matter how many times he was defeated. He always bounced back. Even after a defeat as terrible as the Battle of the Red Cliffs, he still did not fall from power. He had a strong ability to bounce back no matter how many times he was defeated. This must have come from his desire to gather capable people to him.

Cao Cao is known as a cunning hero, so his reputation is a little bit bad. But in some sense, he could be the real hero of *The Records of the Three Kingdoms*. Zhuge Liang and Liu Bei from the Kingdom of Shu are very popular figures. But from another perspective we could say that the idea of the tripartite division of China that Zhuge Liang came up with was unnecessary. This idea ignited an unnecessary war, and the Kingdom of Shu collapsed in the next generation anyway. Without Zhuge Liang's plan, Cao Cao would have been able to unify the kingdoms into one. So we can say that Zhuge Liang hampered him from doing so. In this respect, we could say Zhuge Liang's ability lacked something. Things can be looked at from many different angles in this way.

Using People Working Under You Requires Good Intuition

In order to become a real leader, of course, you need to start with a high level of ability in you. But next, you'll need the ability to use people who are intelligent as your team's "brain." In addition to that, you will also need to set up "generals who are strong in battle," to put it in older terms. In modern terms, the "generals" are the capable sales managers or the star, top-level salespeople. With a highly capable sales team, you can continue selling products one after another, even if they aren't good products. Or, with a highly capable strategy team, you can develop a successful advertising strategy that will create significant exposure and enable you to win a considerable share of the market.

Capable people who rise to leadership have high levels of specialized or sales ability and feel unfulfilled with just winning a bonus as an employee. They're capable of starting a company of their own. If you possess ability in one or another area, your company or wherever you are will grow quickly in the beginning. But at some point, you will face a limit.

To overcome this limit, the support of people with the abilities you don't have is crucial. You will need their advice, and you will need to judge whether you should follow them. For subjects you've never thought about before, you'll require flashes of inspiration, a sense of judgment, and a sense of intuition to determine whether their advice will work or not. Having a wrong sense of intuition isn't good. If your intuition isn't good, you will generally fail at this stage. On the other hand, if your intuition correctly knows when something's right and can predict when something will succeed, you can use capable people even if you, yourself, don't have ability. This is the difficult part.

So, how do you cultivate a correct sense of intuition? First you need to see into the person's true character and ability, even if, you, yourself, can't come up with the same ideas. For example, you have to judge what this person can accomplish when you receive a proposal from him or her or when this person is on the sales team. You need to understand this person's strong points and weak points. You need to judge the level of luck this person possesses and determine whether he or she can win in that kind of situation. You will rise up the ranks if you're capable of judging others' abilities in this way.

So, at first, you need ability as an individual. But later on, that ability won't be enough to let you keep advancing.

Not All Good Baseball Managers Were Originally Star Players

The same can be said in the world of sports. We've seen that star baseball players don't necessarily succeed as baseball managers. For many years, Shigeo Nagashima served as a professional baseball manager, but he didn't succeed at first, even though he had been a star player. The same thing has been true for Sadaharu Oh, who didn't start to shine as a baseball manager until quite some time into his career, even though he had been admired as a "home-run king" as a player.

On the other hand, some baseball managers have gained relative success through methods such as strategic baseball, even though they, themselves, hadn't been star players before. That is to say, they were able to deeply understand the players' inner struggles and hardships. Highly capable people can't help becoming harsh toward others, and they're quickly apt to think, "This person won't do."

A former home-run hitter might look down on a good base-hit player who never hits long balls, thinking, "He's not that great a player, in the end." For example, a home-run hitter might think that someone even like Ichiro, who has a high batting average and a high on-base percentage, is only thinking about hitting grounders, and rarely homers. A home-run hitter might get frustrated watching Ichiro focusing on making the ball bound and fly over the pitcher's head. In this sense, players who specialize at hitting grounders should avoid teams managed by former home-run hitters. Otherwise, they won't become successful. The manager would tell the player to swing harder, and then he'd get fewer hits and his batting average would decline. For this type of player, it's better to get on base somehow, even if he hits grounders, and so I would advise him to go his own way.

In this way, people with high ability aren't guaranteed to succeed as a leader of others. On the other hand, those who have experienced various hardships and thought of many ways to improve themselves can deeply understand the players' feelings and hardships, and because of this, they're capable of guiding them well.

The player's view and the manager's view are a little bit different. To succeed as a leader of many people, you need to have experienced some sadness and suffering. Without this experience, some things will be difficult to understand. Your ability to lead others is related to your ability to understand people's feelings. If what you do goes too smoothly for you, you could often become cold toward others, and then others won't follow your leadership.

The Weak Point in Leaders from Prestigious Families

In addition to overly capable people, people from distinguished and prestigious families need to be handled cautiously. Various prestigious families in Japan come from generation after generation of wealthy or highly intelligent ancestors. Some families have a highly prestigious family history, while other families have fathers, grandfathers, great-grandfathers, and even ancestors from the Edo period who all had a high standing in society.

Be careful when a person from this kind of family background becomes your leader, because there is a cold side to them, after all. They don't feel very appreciative of others. Even if they acknowledge your earnest efforts and hard work, they'll do so only at that time and then forget about it immediately. Since high-status people are overly accustomed to being praised, they don't understand the hard work you had to do to bring them the "prize." You are the hard-working cormorant bird bringing the fisherman your catches of the day. But he might only say, "You caught only 10 fish today? I guess you did so-so," and think no further about your effort. High-status people are like this fisherman who doesn't understand the great favor you did for him.

When an overly capable person or a high-status person becomes your leader, please handle this weak point in them carefully. This is a quality they might have if they were born with talent and smoothly advanced up the ranks or if they have a prestigious family lineage and advanced smoothly due to their parents' influence.

Some politicians come from generation after generation of politicians in their family. Running for election by yourself is difficult if you're from another kind of family, such as a farming family. But if your family background is in politics, you could become a politician in your twenties and a government minister in your forties through your parents' influence. Such people mistake the reason for their success—they think it actually reflects their real ability and will look down on others who are more capable than them. This is how they'll betray you later on, even if you work earnestly to help them. It's a usual aspect of political people you should be aware of if you, yourself, are one or if you're working for one. In addition, you shouldn't overly trust people from generations of royal connections in their family, to put it in olden terms, or who have generation after generation of scholars in their family.

After Age 40, Start Organizing and Leading Others

In this way that I've described, winning by yourself is different from continuing to win with others' assistance. To continually win with others' assistance, you need to gradually start using other people in your work. Please realize that if you have individual ability, you can still fight on your own in your thirties. But you won't be needed if you're fighting in your forties with your individual ability only.

You'll be seen as a burden, as if you're not listening to others and are always playing solo. It becomes a burden to them. It's all right as a younger person, but this won't be appreciated when you are in your forties. At that age, you'll be appreciated more for organizing and leading other people.

If you're working in a large company and fighting based solely on your individual ability, find the right time to move on and start your own business, because otherwise your ability will get buried forever. It's very important to recognize this. It's essential to know that you will be appreciated for a different ability after age 40. It might be something hard to accept, but it's a fact and a truth.

Capture People's Hearts by Developing Your Sensibility

Not the people with high ability in school, but the people who weren't exceptional students become the most widely appreciated as prep school teachers. Usually, since these top-level teachers didn't do so well in their school years, in their continual struggle to do better, they devised their own method of study. A student who scored well using only one widely used textbook or reference book and got admitted easily wouldn't be good at teaching other students how to pass their exams. Such students who become teachers would just say to their students, "You've all read your textbooks, so you should have understood everything." They get bewildered when students don't understand something and think, "Why is this giving them trouble? I explained this part just a few minutes ago, and I explained that part a couple of months ago." It resembles when a star player becomes a baseball manager.

So, actually, the most widely appreciated prep school teachers have spent several post-high school years making further efforts to get admitted. As a result, after overcoming their weakness, they succeeded at getting into a higher-level school than they would have originally. And now, they are teaching the students the method that they managed to devise instead of keeping it to themselves. Then, by continually improving their method, giving it improvement after improvement, they've succeeded at becoming widely appreciated.

In this way, they come to earn salaries as high as 50 to 60 million yen (about 500 to 600 thousand dollars) while the president of Tokyo University earns 20-something million yen a year. Dressed in bow ties and gorgeous clothes, one teacher earns nearly as much as 100 million yen (about 1 million dollars) as he teaches from the front of the classroom. Teachers like him were not exceptional students.

It's indeed a mystery that academically exceptional people end up earning less while some less academically successful people come to earn more. In the end, their higher income is the result of earning widespread appreciation. And it's their own sensibility that helps them earn this appreciation. This sensibility—the ability to appeal to and understand other people's feelings—is also an ability that leads to success in fields such as business.

Unfortunately, a person's sensibility can't be measured by exam scores in school. Schools that specialize in design and music might be able to do so, of course. But otherwise, the sensibilities associated with planning, sales, and marketing can't be measured by exam scores. They cannot be measured by test scores, only by results. So, in the real world, successful people who didn't do exceptionally well in school are highly capable of captivating people's feelings.

So, where does this ability come from? Of course, it comes from your own sufferings and hardships. But first, you must think through your sufferings and hardships, think deeply about them again and again, to create jewel-like pearls within you. You must become like an oyster wrapping shards of sand and glass inside its nacre to produce pearls. You must polish yourself again and again to create pearls within you. Then, after that, you must teach others how to create them as you did.

It's not enough just to suffer. It's not enough just to talk about your suffering, because if you do, people will only run away from you. There's not much value in sharing the story of how you failed. It's just an ordinary story that people don't want to hear.

It's all right to suffer or to fail. But you must grasp something precious or draw something extraordinary from your sufferings and failures. What's important is how deeply people are moved by what you've grasped, how many people's hearts you've captured, how successfully you've led people. It's these things that generate value.

Therefore, if you feel you're not exceptionally intelligent or rational, you should develop your sensibility. There is great power in sensibility. Sensibility can capture the hearts of a great many people.

Sensibility is an ability that is undeniably a part of why great products succeed. No matter how much logic you use, products that don't appeal to people won't sell in the end. You must know that how you polish your sensibility is what sets your capability apart from others'.

4

Think about How to Win with Limited Ability

How Nobunaga Oda Won the Battle of Okehazama

Since this chapter is supposed to be on the theme, "Becoming Invincible," I would like to discuss this topic now. It may sound like I'm exaggerating when I say that you need a battle strategy to succeed in life, but some kind of strategy is indeed necessary. You will need ideas, because if you try to succeed as you now naturally are, you'll become just an ordinary person.

When you are contemplating your strategy, don't overestimate your ability. It's better to assume that your ability is generally limited, that you have limitations. It's essential to think of ways to succeed with little ability. People who believe they're overfilled with so many abilities that they don't know how to use them all cannot develop good strategies. Strategy building is not like that. Instead, it's about devising ways to win with little ability.

In *The Laws of Invincible Leadership*, I explained how Nobunaga Oda (1534–1582) won the Battle of Okehazama (1560). This battle is a long-existing historical topic, and it's been a subject of study by many people indeed. But Nobunaga was actually not the first to put this particular battle tactic to use. Attacking the enemy's middle forces was a long-standing, common-sense battle strategy. Large armies are so huge that the front and back of their regiments are far apart, which makes it difficult for commands to reach those at the end. So by attacking the middle of your enemy's long-stretched forces, you can divide them in half, spread confusion among them, and send them into disarray without their realizing what has happened. Although people say that Nobunaga's surprise tactic was incredible, it was already a rather conventional battle strategy, actually.

It's said that Yoshimoto Imagawa (1519–1560) led a force of 30,000 while Nobunaga led a force of just 2,000 or 3,000. So this battle resembled the Battle of Guandu that I mentioned earlier. Nobunaga faced an enemy ten times the size of his own army, and he needed a way to defeat them.

Imagawa's forces were marching up the Tokaido Road, not a well-maintained road. His army of 30,000 was traveling in a long, snake-like formation, so you can easily estimate its length. While Imagawa and his forces were resting at Okehazama, Nobunaga launched his assault. Only 300 soldiers are said to have been with him at that time. Although, of course, it isn't said by anyone who actually saw them. But it's been said that 300 soldiers were resting and eating there with him.

If Nobunaga's army of 2,000 attacked only these 300 soldiers, he would win without question. Imagawa's forces could total

30,000 soldiers, but this wouldn't matter if Nobunaga was fighting just 300 of them. With 2,000 soldiers, he would win. Nobunaga won a victory he was clearly meant to win.

In battle strategy, it's well-established common sense to attack your enemy's middle forces. In terms of the Three Kingdoms, Liu Bei was defeated by the same battle tactic. When Guan Yu, Liu Bei's sworn brother, suffered defeat, Liu Bei led a counter-attack, again traveling in a long, snake-like formation. Meanwhile, his enemy (from the Kingdom of Wu) was patiently waiting for Liu Bei's army formation to get stretched out, and when it did, they launched a sudden assault on his middle forces. Liu Bei scrambled to escape, barely escaping with his life. But he died shortly afterward.

A large army looks strong, but only in cases when they assault the enemy all at once on flat land. If, instead of that, you let your formation get stretched out too widely while going through mountains, valleys, and narrow paths, your commands won't reach your soldiers. There are cell phones for communication nowadays, but such tools didn't exist at that time, so Liu Bei's forces were defeated in this way.

This battle tactic can also be used when your enemy is crossing a river. By attacking them when half have crossed the river, you will split them in half and throw them into chaos. Your attack will fail if they haven't started crossing the river yet or if all of them have fully finished crossing. But by attacking when half of your enemy has crossed, you could throw them into chaos. You can win with a small army in this way.

Concentrate on Your Opponents' Weak Points

In modern terms, attacking your enemy's middle forces translates like this: A large company's operations get very broad and stretched out into a snake-like formation, like a large army in battle. So the company is unable to develop detailed strategies. As a result, if its core weak point is attacked, it can collapse, guaranteeing its enemy's victory.

For example, a leading Japanese supermarket that used discount tactics was defeated. Various explanations are possible, but the defeat was ultimately due to new companies such as Uniqlo. At a time when the large supermarkets' sales were declining, Uniqlo's sales were multiplying.

How was this possible? Despite the huge risk, Uniqlo moved their entire production line to China, which allowed them to challenge their market with extremely low prices. As a result of that, consumers flocked to Uniqlo stores, resulting in soaring sales growth for Uniqlo even in a time of economic recession, when other businesses were declining.

Why was a discount supermarket defeated by another discount strategy? It was due to the supermarket's overdiversification. When you are in a "snake formation," the executives cannot watch things very closely. This is why you'll be defeated when you face a full-force attack that focuses on one area.

After all is said and done, you cannot win without a strategy. But at the same time, new challengers will defeat you if you become overly comfortable with an existing, successful strategy and you allow it to stay fixed. In such a case, your business's huge growth, itself, will become its fatal wound.

It's impossible to be free of weaknesses as a large business. When your operations move slowly, you will always have areas that are open to attack. They could be your clothing line or your food line. But one of them could become the focus of attack by a challenger who can defeat you, even if you are the leading supermarket chain.

In this way, some large supermarkets and department stores are declining, and convenience stores and other shops using destroyer warship tactics are overtaking them. Small stores like these are now gaining relative popularity. But again, since these stores carry hundreds of different products, specialized businesses such as low-priced hamburger shops and rice bowl shops could challenge these stores' lunch bento market. These specialized places could win these markets by challenging a focused, narrow area.

Large businesses can use strategies for large businesses to win. But until your business grows, your forces need to focus on one area; otherwise, you won't be able to succeed. However large your competitor is, it can't be equally strong in all areas of the market. This means that by focusing your forces and concentrating on challenging your competitor's weak point, you can succeed.

A large business's strength is its abundant variety of products. So, it can be defeated by a challenger selling one focused product. You could defeat a large business by launching a concentrated attack on one market and overtaking the shares there. Then, when your profits increase, they could be used to expand your markets.

But as you do so and as you diversify, new challengers who target your weak points will also appear. Again and again, this kind of process repeats itself in the world of business. But ultimately, you will always need to think of concentrating your forces if your business doesn't have a lot of power yet. Otherwise, you'll get defeated.

Your College Admissions Strategy Should Involve Narrowing Your Focus

The same is true when you're studying for exams. By stretching yourself too broadly, you could falter. A Japanese student's college admissions preparation lasts one to three years. Your success depends on what you do with this period, and you could fail if you stretch yourself too broadly.

If you ask your smart friends about the method they're using, one may say, "I use this reference book." Another may say, "I've been taking classes at this cram school," and still another may say, "I'm using this workbook." Everyone will tell you something different. But if you try everything, you won't have enough time and you could fail. So, passing a college examination depends on what you focus on within your given time.

During such a time, you won't succeed if you spread your subjects out too much or attempt overly advanced or overly high-level things. For example, you might think of studying your aspirational university's classroom textbooks, thinking the admissions exams are created by the professors there. You may think you'll score better on your exam by doing so. But it wouldn't matter how many years you studied those textbooks, you still wouldn't pass the exam. You might think that by studying some subjects ahead, you will get an advantage, but you'd be wasting time studying materials that won't be on your exam. By studying materials that are more advanced than other students', you will end up not passing the exam.

You might feel sad about accepting your limited ability and focusing just on areas where you have the highest chances of success. But it's what you must do. Your chances for success are higher if you study one workbook three times than if you were to study three different ones only once.

If teachers advise reading the English newspaper word for word, don't take this advice to heart. If you do, you could spend ten years reading newspapers and still fail the exam. Imagine how many words are used in English newspapers. Tens of thousands or even more than a hundred thousand English words are used in them. Even if you're advised to read *Time* magazine and *Newsweek* magazine, they use more than 100,000 English words. But you only need to know 5,000 English words to pass the college entrance exam.

You don't have time to learn unnecessary words. Instead, you need to study the English words on the test; otherwise, you won't pass it. Unnecessary effort like this happens a lot. So be cautious about accepting other people's advice. Consider the practicality of their advice for your aim. If they're not practical for your aim, sometimes it's better not to follow them. In this sense, it's essential to always look at the time given to you and check to see if you are spreading yourself too thin or aiming too high.

In addition, it's better for some people to apply to a national public university, while a private university is better for others. Which person you are depends on how you estimate yourself at the beginning. If you are very confident, you might study all five subjects and apply to a national university. And in case you don't get accepted into that one, you could also apply to a private university as back-up, based on three subjects. It all depends on how you foresee your final level of academic ability, the level you'll succeed at developing by the time of your exam.

Someone might say, "Studying all five subjects is too hard for you, and you won't get into a national university anyway. So don't aim to do that. Abandon two of the five subjects from the start to concentrate on three subjects. By narrowing down to three subjects, you can aim for the same level of school as a smart student studying all five. So, don't apply to a national university. It's not worth applying to one just for the sake of applying." If someone gives you straight, hard advice like this, you might get admitted by a private university. Your mentor might say, "You won't get into a national university, so don't bother applying to one." "Among the universities for the three subjects, this one's exam covers less material, so apply to this one." "Don't apply to this university, because their English exam has extremely long reading comprehension questions." "This is the only university with a true-or-false exam, so you could pass theirs easily." "This school's social studies questions are memorization-based and only come from such-and-such area. With this university, you could easily narrow down the materials you'll need to study."

By keeping your mind open, following this mentor's advice, and narrowing down what you'll do, you might succeed at getting accepted. But if you spread yourself too thin, you won't pass the exam no matter how hard you try. And when you fail, you'll put in further effort and spread yourself even thinner, which won't do you much good.

Bravely Throw Away Inessentials

Having an all-in mentality is all right. Still, you should stop yourself at some point. You should abandon things that you feel you shouldn't do. But this is a very difficult thing to make yourself do. When you follow your desires, you feel anxious and end up studying more materials.

It takes courage to stop yourself, but this courage is connected to your wisdom. You need courage to bravely throw away what's inessential for you.

This is also related to your work. Don't overly spread yourself out in your work. Sometimes, less-intelligent people spend much of their time on trivial things, as a warm-up, before finally getting to their main work. They can't immediately get themselves to work on their main work, so they work on less-important, peripheral things, believing they'll eventually feel motivated and something will inspire them. They kill time in this way.

You can't win in this way. To attack the main job, it's crucial to concentrate just on this main, difficult job. To succeed, plan some kind of strategy, whether by dividing it into smaller tasks or asking for support. It's essential to do so.

5

Use Conventional Methods to Fight and Win Battles You Can Win

Winning a Long War Requires Sufficient Military Forces

I also talked about detour tactics in *The Laws of Invincible Leadership*, but it's very difficult to use these tactics successfully. If you could execute a skillful detour tactic, you would succeed brilliantly. But if you are not so intelligent and were to employ it, you might end up never achieving your goal. Without a deep understanding of your own capability, you might end up not reaching your destination. This really happens to people. It's really true.

If you are someone who's capable of getting straight to the target and winning that battle, then using a detour tactic once in a while could help you win a victory. But if you're someone who's always taking detours, it might just mean that you're slow, so please be careful. The best way to win is to take the most traditional route, the shortest distance to your goal, and get there in the shortest amount of time.

In a war, you'll never win the final victory if you are always focused on being the weak side challenging the strong enemy. This may be fine in the beginning, but you must become the stronger side eventually. And when you do, it's essential to change your battle strategy to the kind that leads the strong side to win as a strong side. This is the traditional textbook strategy.

But some people are exceptionally strong in battle and sometimes can win by using detour tactics. I mentioned the example of Yoshitsune Minamoto (1159–1189) in *The Laws of Invincible Leadership*. In the Battle of Ichinotani, in Hiyodorigoe, which is present-day Suma ward in Kobe City, Yoshitsune led a few dozen cavalrymen down a mountain path, assaulting the Heike clan's base camp. The exact size of the Heike clan's army is not known, but I'm sure it couldn't easily be beaten by just a few dozen cavalrymen. Yet, when the Heike clan saw their head camp, of all places, get assaulted and set on fire, they were caught completely by surprise and were defeated.

Yoshitsune succeeded in this tactic, but we don't know if someone else would have also succeeded. It's definitely possible that while riding down the mountain, their leader and his horse could have fallen and died. Such an accident happening would have meant their failure right then. Or, if the enemy had a good military advisor who foresaw the possibility of an imminent attack, men armed with spears would have been stationed at the foot of the mountain. If this had happened, Yoshitsune's men would have been completely defeated instantly. Everyone would have died.

Gambles like this are a part of detour tactics. As another example, when he was going to the Heike clan's camp in Yashima,

Kagawa prefecture, Yoshitsune chose a stormy day to cross the sea. After landing his ship in Katsuura, Tokushima prefecture, he borrowed horses and troops from influential local clans and marched northward to Yashima, assaulting his enemy from behind. This was another attack when Yoshitsune used a surprise assault to lead a small army to victory.

The Heike clan thought his attack would come by sea and were paying attention only to the ocean. The Heike clan was excellent in naval warfare, had many ships, and had control of much of the sea. Yoshitsune's Minamoto Clan only had a few ships, so the Heike clan never expected defeat to be possible. They were confident they'd win. So when they saw Yoshitsune's assault coming from the land behind them instead of the sea, the Heike clan was caught completely off guard, and they scrambled in confusion as they fled to Dannoura.

Yoshitsune's assault succeeded. But whether an average leader would have succeeded is uncertain. People around Yoshitsune didn't want him to cross the sea during a storm. If his ship sinks in the storm, the attack will fail right then. So it was only natural they'd want to stop him. Although the storm would keep him and his army hidden from the enemy's eyes, it was also a huge risk.

In these ways I've just talked about, Yoshitsune won battles. Because of them in Japanese history, the Imperial Japanese military focused on studying their battle tactics. They always studied episodes of weak forces winning against strong forces and frequently used surprise tactics. But when it becomes a long-term war, the stronger force is bound to win. You cannot depend on only battle tactics to win a war for this reason. When the difference in skills, military forces, and food is great, you will lose in the final analysis. You need to know this. In the end, you cannot win without a strong military.

Failing to See the Usefulness of Radar Technology, Japan Was Defeated by Strategy

In World War II, Japan, a country that was strong in naval warfare, was defeated in a naval battle by the United States. To reach Japan, the U.S. naval fleet traveled a long distance across the Pacific Ocean. It was a difficult journey, and they understood that fighting the Japanese would not be easy. On top of that, unlike the Japanese who had fought in wars before, the Americans hadn't experienced many wars and were unused to fighting one. Considering these things and the long distance the Americans had traveled, they, for a fact, were weak. So Japan's defeat against the U.S. was, in fact, due to a defeat in the area of strategy.

I wrote in *The Laws of Invincible Leadership* that one reason for Japan's defeat was the U.S.'s use of radar technology. Japan also had developed their own radar technology, actually, even before the Americans had. But the Japanese leaders hadn't understood the usefulness of this technology.

The Japanese warships had radar on them, but it was of very poor quality and didn't function properly. This was why they thought that their own eyesight was better, that if they could train to have 3.0 vision, they'd be able to see farther distances. So, the Japanese also had radar technology, but it wasn't more effective than human eyesight because of its poor quality.

Also, since it broke down frequently, they found human eyesight much more reliable. Since some African tribes have people with 8.0 vision, maybe the Japanese tried training their eyes to have animal-hunting vision. But it's clear that they still wouldn't have won against the American's well-functioning radar technology.

Japan was defeated in the Battle of the Philippine Sea, led by commander-in-chief Jisaburo Ozawa, who out of sheer will adopted the "Outrange Strategy." The Japanese aircraft carriers' air corps were said to have an attack radius of about 740 kilometers, and the American air corps had an attack radius of 460 kilometers. In a battle between aircraft carriers, the Japanese commander said that they would definitely win decisively if they kept a set distance from the enemy. The Japanese air corps would still be capable of attacking the Americans. This was called the "Outrange Strategy." He thought that by launching an attack from the farthest distance possible, his air corps can launch an attack on the Americans and return without giving them an opportunity to counterattack. He imagined that this would allow them to fight one-sidedly and win.

But the high-quality radar equipment on the American fleet indicated when the Japanese forces were attacking, making this distance meaningless. The American air corps only needed to attack by waiting from a higher altitude than the Japanese planes when they came. So the Americans were able to shoot down the Japanese planes one by one, leading to Japan's defeat in the war.

This was a defeat in battle strategy. The Japanese tried to take advantage of their larger attack-range radius to win the battle. But in order to actually win a victory, they needed a different strategy, because radar was being used. Only, their commander's awareness of radar technology's usefulness wasn't enough.

By contrast, the Americans' battle strategy demonstrated significant foresight. Sixty years after the war, their strategy basically hasn't changed even now. The flagship of the U.S. Seventh Fleet headquartered in Yokosuka, Japan, is not a warship right now. It is not armed with a lot of weapons. It doesn't carry any cannons or missiles. In a sense, it's a small command and control vessel directing the fleet through intelligence and communications only. It's like an advanced radar system concept. The fleet's flagship, which serves as its headquarters, only houses this intelligence and communication system.

Ultimately, Japan's focus on warship strategy was behind the times. Even though Japan had an exceptional strategy for aircraft carriers in their Pearl Harbor attack, they couldn't foresee what would happen after that.

In this way, when you win a victory, sometimes you don't realize how to develop your strategy more to gain further victory. Meanwhile, other smart people learn from this successful strategy and copy it, gaining the advantage against you. When highly intelligent people see your strategy, they could learn from your success as a case study for themselves. They'll copy your small success and use it against you to defeat you later. For this reason, maintaining successful tactics and battle strategies can be very difficult to do.

Heihachiro Togo's Battle Strategy That Won against the Russian Baltic Fleet

Learning from the past is important. But be aware that there are also ways of fighting which no one has thought of yet. For example, there is the battle strategy called "Crossing the T," that Admiral Heihachiro Togo devised to defeat the Russian Baltic Fleet. The Russian Fleet had been traveling in two vertical lines, side by side. Conventionally, the opposing sides faced forward and fired at each other. But most of the ammunition each side fired didn't reach the opposing sides. What the Japanese fleet did was turn their ships around so that the longer sides faced the front of their Russian ships, forming the letter T. Since this battle strategy made it easier for the enemy to fire at them, the majority of people resisted it. In particular, they'd be put in the greatest danger while they were turning the ships. They were afraid that exposing more of their ships would make them easier to fire at, and they could end up sinking.

But this strategy could be looked at another way. The conventional formation allowed them to use the guns only on the front of the ship. By facing the long side to their enemy however, all of the ship's guns on the front, back, and the long sides would become usable. This would let them outnumber the Russians' guns, giving the Japanese a chance to destroy the Russian ship if skilled artillery men are firing them. Indeed, it would have been difficult to forecast who will be destroyed, you or the enemy. If you were the commander or the naval advisor, what would you have decided on? Which side would you have thought will win? In the face of an enemy coming at you in vertical formation, you are about to turn your broadside to fire at each other. Do you think you would win, or do you think your enemy would win?

You, who have the larger amount of exposed surface area, could be an easier target. That is one thing to consider. If your enemy is using skilled artillerymen, you might suffer many hits. Since you cannot shoot at your enemy while you're turning your ship sideways, it's possible that you might get shot to destruction. On the other hand, with more usable guns to shoot at your enemy with, you could be the one to win.

In the actual battle, the Russian Baltic Fleet was almost completely destroyed by this maneuver, resulting in Japan's victory. Sometimes, it is also called an alpha-maneuver in foreign records, because the maneuver seemed to draw the letter α. This was the battle strategy Heihachiro Togo used. In reality, he wasn't the first to use this maneuver—it was a strategy that had been used in

Japanese naval battles of older times. Naval forces in older Japanese history, such as the Murakami and Kuki naval forces, had used this strategy, and Heihachiro Togo's naval adviser, Saneyuki Akiyama, had studied these battles.

But getting too immersed in battle strategy could also lead you to defeat. So, it's very difficult to forecast who will win. It's your sense of intuition here that will determine your fate as a leader.

6

Ultimately, Fight with Your Actual Capability

In this chapter, I've talked about various topics. If you go on as you are now, you can only win with your limited innate ability. So if you want to gain greater victory, you will indeed need to make an effort. You will need to use all of your human knowledge possible as you make this effort. If you know a way to win that your opponent hasn't thought about yet, a complete victory is possible.

Often, we fail when we feel a worldly desire to win and we try to do too many things. So, it's indeed when you feel this desire to win that you should recognize the limits of your ability, narrow your focus, and think about how to win.

It's essential to know that surprise tactics are a way of fighting local battles. But when you look at how life flows as a whole, you must know that those who should win will win, and those who should be defeated will be defeated. This is how the flow of life goes.

Ultimately, it's important to think about how to fight within your capability. Things won't go so well unless you're able to objectively calculate the level of your own actual capability and the kind of results that your efforts and ingenuity will create for you. The element of surprise and surprise tactics might be needed sometimes. But, on the whole, it's indeed important to use conventional methods to win victories. It's because you have been winning by using conventional strategy, that you're sometimes able to surprise your opponent and achieve great success using surprise tactics. If you are always using surprise tactics, they will expect that and prepare themselves for it, so your tactics will end up failing.

It's admirable for the weak to defeat the strong. But you shouldn't be attached to being small. If you are too absorbed in tactics, you will want to remain small forever, in the end. To become successful, you will first need to win a victory. But once you've succeeded and grown further, don't stay too absorbed in the tactics. This is a time when you have to change the way you fight; you now need to fight as someone who has become strong.

I've discussed the theme of "Becoming Invincible" over the course of this chapter. After all is said and done, the first stepping stone is some level of knowledge. If someone has already experienced something you haven't experienced yet, borrow from their knowledge and think whether it's something you could make use of for yourself. It may or may not succeed as you would like it to. But with each try, your senses will heighten, and the number of your successes will steadily grow. At Happy Science, we also teach various ways of devising strategies; for example, we offer teachings on management. By studying them and making them your own, I'm sure you can open a new path for yourself.

NOTES

1   See Ryuho Okawa, *Invincible Thinking* (New York: IRH Press, 2017). See page 220 for more information on this book.

CHAPTER FIVE

Fulfill Your Mission of Light

Filling This Earth with Light

1

Do You Have a Burning Desire with a Sense of Mission?

Your Life's Mission to Shed Light upon the World

This chapter is a message about my hopes for the times ahead. I wish I could give a message directly to each of you, one by one. But because I cannot, I hope this written message conveys my true feelings to a great many of you.

I wish for you all to take these words to heart: "Fulfill your mission of light." Please impress them into your heart deeply. As long as we look objectively at the world's situation, countless things indeed seem impossible or improbable. When you look at your surroundings for reasons you cannot do something, they number endlessly. Any number of excuses can let us say, "I can't because of this" or "I couldn't because of that."

I'm sure they're not untrue and it's just as you say. But another truth is that winds in this world and our lives are not always favorable. But if you can't move ahead unless the winds are favorable for you, then you're being much too frail and undependable.

Whether the winds are favorable, against you, or calm, the feeling inside you that says, "It doesn't matter. I will still fulfill my mission of light anyway," is important. So, first, please ask yourself, "Do I feel a burning desire with a sense of mission?" Please begin by asking this question.

Indeed, there will be countless objectively bad conditions and circumstances. When they come, look inside yourself and check for a burning desire for your mission first. Is the fire of your torch burning? Is the flame of your inner candle alight? Checking yourself this way is important indeed. As long as this fire, this light, keeps burning, you can continue walking ahead. As long as this light burns, you cannot help but move forward day by day, whatever the day brings you. Whether stormy weather, pouring rain, blustering winds, or storming snow come to you, you can, indeed, keep going, because you'll know it's your mission to shed light upon the world.

The World around You
Is Really Overfilled with Light

Most of this earthly world's unhappiness comes from self-concentrated thinking. If light is fulfilling its mission of light through your self-concentrated thinking, then it's not a problem, of course. But if this world gets overfilled by people who shout in the darkness of their ignorance, "There is no light," and demand others to bring them light, then this world will become a Hell.

Imagine such a situation. For example, imagine the middle of a war zone. Such a situation would feel like you're inside a Hell.

It would also feel this way in a storm of economic recessions and business bankruptcies. It would also feel this way in times of many family illnesses or repeating misfortunes among your relatives. These are situations without light.

In the midst of them, it's possible to grumble and to complain to others. You can blame society, politicians, and anything else. And you'll also have opportunities to voice these feelings. Sometimes, they'll be righteous feelings.

But before doing so, examine and check inside yourself for something you've not done yet. You must begin there. Most people in lightless circumstances are saying, "Give me light. I want light." It's something we call selfish, self-preserving desires.

There indeed is light. It just seems as if there isn't because something's covering it.

You can indeed burn your inner light in your current circumstances. If this sounds untrue, then think of someone else in the same bad situation, or at the bottom of his or her life, or even worse than that, who lived in dedication to others and the world anyway. When feeling ill, ask yourself if someone with a worse illness or in worse physical condition made efforts anyway. When doing poorly in school, ask if there are others like you who have put in more effort and perseverance than you have. When these people are counted up, they'll number endlessly.

It's the same with family problems. I'm sure you have dissatisfactions. I'm sure that you have worries and that your income, brothers and sisters, and parents' personalities dissatisfy you. I'm sure you'll face such kind of problems. But how about people without any family? How about people who no longer have an income? Your workplace might feel dissatisfying, but it could be far more blessed than a bedridden patient's circumstances.

You may think that you're in the worst circumstances and you deserve sympathy, but you must realize that this isn't actually so. Your life is overfilled with light in the eyes of people going through much greater suffering. You just haven't noticed that.

An Abundance of Choices Is the Real Cause of Affluent Societies' Worries

What is the real source of your worries and sufferings, then? They mostly come from the wealth of available choices. This makes up most of people's worries in an abundant society. There are so many choices. There is this choice and that choice. With so many choices available, you think that making the best choices you would like to will give you a chance at great success. So, when things don't go how you would like them to, you worry. Most worries are blessed ones like that.

Many of you see these blessed worries as true worries. But people around the world live without any choices in their circumstances. Japan may have poor classroom conditions, bad schoolteachers, or disruptive home environments for children trying to study.

But missiles are flying overhead and flying ammunition surrounds people elsewhere in the world. What thoughts are going through these people's minds? They are hoping they can reopen their classrooms even a day sooner. They're wishing for peaceful days to return so they can study again.

It's said that we are in a recession in Japan. But is this true in the eyes of the rest of the world? In Japan, people's lives are many times, or even tens of times, more abundant than people's lives in other countries. Is Japan truly in an economic recession, then?

Many people also complain that they don't get any help from the government. But is this true? Japanese people get various kinds of thorough government services. And all developed countries' politics are very kind to the weak; they provide various social services to their people. Developed countries give their people an unimaginable level of help compared to developing countries. But people of developed countries keep complaining and seeking more, saying, "I want more. Give me more." And more people are not trying to stand on their own feet, not making their own efforts, and complaining more and voicing dissatisfactions more because of such abundant government protection and assistance.

I would like such people to go back to the starting point. For a time, the world may seem to go into recession or to regress decades backwards due to economic decline. But this teaches you to reflect on whether you have been saying things selfishly, being extravagant, and overly relying on the help of others. It's teaching you to go back to the starting point of being human and to do the things you should do and make efforts.

Adversity Is a Precious Chance to Polish Your Soul

You don't get success in only easygoing circumstances. You also get success from difficulties, because being born to this earthly world itself asks for a lot of trials. If everything in your life went exactly as you would like it to, smoothly and without difficulty, and you were able to succeed and return to the other world, then you would regret most things. You would realize that you didn't have enough hardships, even though you came to this third-dimensional, material world of difficulties. You'd regret wasting the precious opportunity to persevere through adversities that polish your soul. You'd feel this complete opposite feeling from what you felt while you were in this world.

Even though you feel as if you're suffering in this world, your soul is getting polished at this time. The greater your soul's mission is, the greater your adversities may be. This is why you can tell the capacity of your soul from the adversities you face. Doing so is important. If great adversity comes to you, you must think that this is showing how great your mission is. You must think that you are now polishing your soul, that you're given a workbook of life's problems for polishing your soul.

So, read the will of the being who gave this workbook of problems to you by looking at the contents inside it. Then, think about what you must do.

2

What Can You Do
in Your Circumstances Now?

Accumulate Efforts
and Get Stronger Willpower

In the beginning of this chapter, I talked about lighting a fire in your heart, lighting the fire of your inner torch, lighting the fire of your inner candle. The first important thing in doing so is awakening to a sense of mission. Second, the strong will you build from this sense of mission is indeed, important.

But you won't succeed so easily by trying to suddenly strengthen your will. Because of our human weakness, our New Year's resolutions usually crumble before even a week goes by.

Like our physical muscles, a strong will doesn't come from sudden training. Suddenly lifting tens of kilograms of heavy rocks or heavy weights won't create stronger muscles instantly. You might end up hurting yourself in the end, and you won't be able to exercise for a while. Or you might even need to go to the hospital. Your muscles need to get trained through various daily exercises that gradually strengthen them. This is how they get stronger. Resolving suddenly, one day, to do something is the same as suddenly lifting up a gigantic rock; you could hurt yourself straightaway, and that would be the end of that.

Your will gets trained the same way your muscles get trained. It's important to accumulate efforts steadily in practical ways. By doing so, a level of actual ability develops in you, and you will gain the kind of strong power that doesn't get easily discouraged by slight hardships and difficulties. Please think that training daily is essential.

So, strong willpower that you get from your sense of mission is essential. And to get strong willpower, you need training.

Take Definite Steps Forward Where You Are Now

A practical mindset and taking sure steps forward, one by one, are important, too. Take sure steps forward in your circumstances now. Your way forward lies not in relying on God or Buddha for everything, but in doing what you can, no matter how small it could be. Do things that help society, help family, help your school, help your workplace, and help yourself in the true sense. Make efforts to accumulate one such deed and then another. This is so essential to do.

I said in this book's prologue that prayer is extremely important. But I'm not encouraging a mindset of relying completely on outside power in an easygoing way.

You should go to God or the high spirits when there is nothing further your power can do. As a human being, you cannot help but turn to God in such times. I'm certain you will need to do so to get peace of mind.

But if you're physically strong enough to be active in this earthly world, it's much too early to say that you can't. Have strong willpower, and think about what you must do where you are standing now. What can you do? Instead of thinking about what you will do in more fortunate circumstances, think about what you can do where you are standing now.

There is no such thing as nothing. There is always something you can do. This something is your mission of light. Think, "I can fulfill my mission of light even in these circumstances, now. How can I fulfill it?" You can fulfill it even while lying in a hospital bed. You can fulfill it even if you're sick, whether you're a nurse, a doctor, a schoolteacher, a student, a construction worker, a government official, a fishmonger, a grocer, a factory worker, or someone of any other occupation; whoever you are, it doesn't matter. You can still progress another step in your mission.

Think that the circumstances and standing you are given now are connected to your true life and your life's workbook of problems. If your workbook now is too easy to solve, more difficult problems will appear. If your workbook now is too difficult, the problems will eventually get easier. But don't grumble about your workbook of problems. Instead, think about doing what you should do right now.

When numerous people wish to light up their own light, this earthly world will overfill with light and get closer to Heaven. But if more people ask to get help from others, then this world will sink into darkness.

Remove the Obstruction in Your Mind That's Blocking the Light

God's power is great. God's light is gigantic. It is like the sun that sends tremendous energy into the universe. The sun's energy is incredible. But a hat or a single sheet of cardboard can obstruct it. Even then, the sun's light itself isn't weak. Its energy is tremendous, reaching all of the universe, bringing daylight and nourishment to animals and plants. It has an incredible power.

But a hat or a sheet of cardboard can easily obstruct it, leading to shadows. This hat or sheet of cardboard are the sufferings and hardships disrupting your life right now. Even such things can create shadows. Your present state of suffering is like those shadows. They are the Hell you are creating yourself.

But they cannot truly compete with sunlight's energy. Your sufferings and hardships are just trifles. They only seem as if they're obstructing the sunshine, just for a time. They are not truly realities. You must try to see through what these obstructions are. They are truly something silly, something simple, something that one hand can remove.

It only seems as if they are big enough to compete with the sun. But it's truly foolish to think that they really are.

Usually, they are created in your mind. These obstructions are things you, yourself, are creating—which means that you have power to take them away. It's not difficult to do. It's not a huge darkness, obstruction, or adversity.

First, you must want to try. You must want to do so. You must try to fulfill your mission of light. You will take your first step when you think of doing so. A child as a child, a mother as a mother, a husband as a husband, a superior as a superior, and a subordinate as a subordinate have their missions to fulfill.

Please firstly fulfill your mission of light. We will make these words, "Fulfill your mission of light," our slogan as we go forward together.

Afterword

This book is full of courage, wisdom, and light. This Laws Series' eleventh book reflects my renewed aim to become the Light lighting up the world. It's truly my wish to give all people hope. It's truly my wish for people's delight to be my delight and for people's happiness to be my happiness.

This book, *The Laws of Hope*, itself, is my love for all of you. O you, who have worries, stand up. O you, who are suffering, you will get courage from me. Now with you, here in Japan, here on this globe of Earth, is this Light. I dare ask you to spread this gospel of hope.

Ryuho Okawa
Master and CEO of Happy Science Group
January 1, 2006

The LAWS *of* HOPE

This book is a compilation of the lectures as listed below.

- PROLOGUE -

ON HOPE

Japanese title: *Kibo ni Tsuite*

Lecture released on December 4, 2005

- CHAPTER ONE -

TRY TO PRAISE YOURSELF MORE

Japanese title: *Jibun wo Motto Hometemiyou*

Lecture released on October 2, 2005

- CHAPTER TWO -

WHAT IT MEANS TO SUCCEED

Japanese title: *Seikou Suru to Iu Koto*

Lecture released on February 3, 2002

- CHAPTER THREE -
SUCCESS THAT PREVAILS
FROM THIS WORLD TO THE OTHER WORLD

Japanese title: *Konoyo to Anoyo wo Tsuranuku Seikou*

Lecture released on December 2004 ~ March 2005

- CHAPTER FOUR -
BECOMING INVINCIBLE

Japanese title: *Josho no Hito to Naru Tame niwa*

Lecture released on May 1, 2002

- CHAPTER FIVE -
FULFILL YOUR MISSION OF LIGHT

Japanese title: *Hikari no Shimei wo Hatase*

Lecture released on January 1, 2004

ABOUT THE AUTHOR

RYUHO OKAWA was born on July 7th 1956, in Tokushima, Japan. After graduating from the University of Tokyo with a law degree, he joined a Tokyo-based trading house. While working at its New York headquarters, he studied international finance at the Graduate Center of the City University of New York. In 1981, he attained Great Enlightenment and became aware that he is El Cantare with a mission to bring salvation to all humankind. In 1986, he established Happy Science. It now has members in over 140 countries across the world, with more than 700 local branches and temples as well as 10,000 missionary houses around the world. The total number of lectures has exceeded 3,200 (of which more than 150 are in English) and over 2,750 books (of which more than 550 are Spiritual Interview Series) have been published, many of which are translated into 31 languages. Many of the books, including *The Laws of the Sun* have become best sellers or million sellers. To date, Happy Science has produced 21 movies. The original story and original concept were given by the Executive Producer Ryuho Okawa. Recent movie titles are *Living in the Age of Miracles* (documentary, Aug. 2020), *Twiceborn* (live-action, Oct.2020), and *Beautiful Lure–A Modern Tale of "Painted Skin"* (live-action movie scheduled to be released in May 2021). He has also composed the lyrics and music of over 200 songs, such as theme songs and featured songs of movies. Moreover, he is the Founder of Happy Science University and Happy Science Academy (Junior and Senior High School), Founder and President of the Happiness Realization Party, Founder and Honorary Headmaster of Happy Science Institute of Government and Management, Founder of IRH Press Co., Ltd., and the Chairperson of New Star Production Co., Ltd. and ARI Production Co., Ltd.

WHAT IS EL CANTARE?

El Cantare means "the Light of the Earth," and is the Supreme God of the Earth who has been guiding humankind since the beginning of Genesis. He is whom Jesus called Father and Muhammad called Allah. Different parts of El Cantare's core consciousness have descended to Earth in the past, once as Alpha and another as Elohim. His branch spirits, such as Shakyamuni Buddha and Hermes, have descended to Earth many times and helped to flourish many civilizations. To unite various religions and to integrate various fields of study in order to build a new civilization on Earth, a part of the core consciousness has descended to Earth as Master Ryuho Okawa.

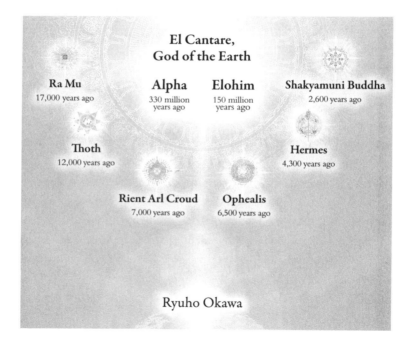

El Cantare, God of the Earth

Ra Mu
17,000 years ago

Alpha
330 million years ago

Elohim
150 million years ago

Shakyamuni Buddha
2,600 years ago

Thoth
12,000 years ago

Hermes
4,300 years ago

Rient Arl Croud
7,000 years ago

Ophealis
6,500 years ago

Ryuho Okawa

Alpha is a part of the core consciousness of El Cantare who descended to Earth around 330 million years ago. Alpha preached Earth's Truths to harmonize and unify Earth-born humans and space people who came from other planets.

Elohim is a part of El Cantare's core consciousness who descended to Earth around 150 million years ago. He gave wisdom, mainly on the differences of light and darkness, good and evil.

Shakyamuni Buddha was born as a prince into the Shakya Clan in India around 2,600 years ago. When he was 29 years old, he renounced the world and sought enlightenment. He later attained Great Enlightenment and founded Buddhism.

Hermes is one of the 12 Olympian gods in Greek mythology, but the spiritual Truth is that he taught the teachings of love and progress around 4,300 years ago that became the origin of the current Western civilization. He is a hero that truly existed.

Ophealis was born in Greece around 6,500 years ago and was the leader who took an expedition to as far as Egypt. He is the God of miracles, prosperity, and arts, and is known as Osiris in the Egyptian mythology.

Rient Arl Croud was born as a king of the ancient Incan Empire around 7,000 years ago and taught about the mysteries of the mind. In the heavenly world, he is responsible for the interactions that take place between various planets.

Thoth was an almighty leader who built the golden age of the Atlantic civilization around 12,000 years ago. In the Egyptian mythology, he is known as god Thoth.

Ra Mu was a leader who built the golden age of the civilization of Mu around 17,000 years ago. As a religious leader and a politician, he ruled by uniting religion and politics.

ABOUT HAPPY SCIENCE

Happy Science is a global movement that empowers individuals to find purpose and spiritual happiness and to share that happiness with their families, societies, and the world. With more than 12 million members around the world, Happy Science aims to increase awareness of spiritual truths and expand our capacity for love, compassion, and joy so that together we can create the kind of world we all wish to live in.

Activities at Happy Science are based on the Principles of Happiness (Love, Wisdom, Self-Reflection, and Progress). These principles embrace worldwide philosophies and beliefs, transcending boundaries of culture and religions.

> **Love** teaches us to give ourselves freely without expecting anything in return; it encompasses giving, nurturing, and forgiving.

> **Wisdom** leads us to the insights of spiritual truths, and opens us to the true meaning of life and the will of God (the universe, the highest power, Buddha).

> **Self-Reflection** brings a mindful, nonjudgmental lens to our thoughts and actions to help us find our truest selves—the essence of our souls—and deepen our connection to the highest power. It helps us attain a clean and peaceful mind and leads us to the right life path.

Progress emphasizes the positive, dynamic aspects of our spiritual growth—actions we can take to manifest and spread happiness around the world. It's a path that not only expands our soul growth, but also furthers the collective potential of the world we live in.

PROGRAMS AND EVENTS

The doors of Happy Science are open to all. We offer a variety of programs and events, including self-exploration and self-growth programs, spiritual seminars, meditation and contemplation sessions, study groups, and book events.

Our programs are designed to:
* Deepen your understanding of your purpose and meaning in life
* Improve your relationships and increase your capacity to love unconditionally
* Attain peace of mind, decrease anxiety and stress, and feel positive
* Gain deeper insights and a broader perspective on the world
* Learn how to overcome life's challenges
  ... and much more.

*For more information, visit **happy-science.org**.*

CONTACT INFORMATION

Happy Science is a worldwide organization with faith centers around the globe. For a comprehensive list of centers, visit the worldwide directory at *happy-science.org*. The following are some of the many Happy Science locations:

UNITED STATES AND CANADA

New York
79 Franklin St., New York, NY 10013
Phone: 212-343-7972
Fax: 212-343-7973
Email: ny@happy-science.org
Website: happyscience-na.org

New Jersey
725 River Rd, #102B, Edgewater, NJ 07020
Phone: 201-313-0127
Fax: 201-313-0120
Email: nj@happy-science.org
Website: happyscience-na.org

Florida
5208 8th St., St. Zephyrhills, FL 33542
Phone: 813-715-0000
Fax: 813-715-0010
Email: florida@happy-science.org
Website: happyscience-na.org

Atlanta
1874 Piedmont Ave., NE Suite 360-C
Atlanta, GA 30324
Phone: 404-892-7770
Email: atlanta@happy-science.org
Website: happyscience-na.org

San Francisco
525 Clinton St.
Redwood City, CA 94062
Phone & Fax: 650-363-2777
Email: sf@happy-science.org
Website: happyscience-na.org

Los Angeles
1590 E. Del Mar Blvd., Pasadena, CA 91106
Phone: 626-395-7775
Fax: 626-395-7776
Email: la@happy-science.org
Website: happyscience-na.org

Orange County
10231 Slater Ave., #204
Fountain Valley, CA 92708
Phone: 714-745-1140
Email: oc@happy-science.org
Website: happyscience-na.org

San Diego
7841 Balboa Ave., Suite #202
San Diego, CA 92111
Phone: 626-395-7775
Fax: 626-395-7776
E-mail: sandiego@happy-science.org
Website: happyscience-na.org

Hawaii
Phone: 808-591-9772
Fax: 808-591-9776
Email: hi@happy-science.org
Website: happyscience-na.org

Kauai
3343 Kanakolu Street, Suite 5
Lihue, HI 96766, U.S.A.
Phone: 808-822-7007
Fax: 808-822-6007
Email: kauai-hi@happy-science.org
Website: kauai.happyscience-na.org

Toronto

845 The Queensway
Etobicoke ON M8Z 1N6 Canada
Phone: 1-416-901-3747
Email: toronto@happy-science.org
Website: happy-science.ca

INTERNATIONAL

Tokyo

1-6-7 Togoshi, Shinagawa
Tokyo, 142-0041 Japan
Phone: 81-3-6384-5770
Fax: 81-3-6384-5776
Email: tokyo@happy-science.org
Website: happy-science.org

London

3 Margaret St.
London,W1W 8RE United Kingdom
Phone: 44-20-7323-9255
Fax: 44-20-7323-9344
Email: eu@happy-science.org
Website: happyscience-uk.org

Sydney

516 Pacific Hwy, Lane Cove North,
NSW 2066, Australia
Phone: 61-2-9411-2877
Fax: 61-2-9411-2822
Email: sydney@happy-science.org

Brazil Headquarters

Rua. Domingos de Morais 1154,
Vila Mariana, Sao Paulo SP
CEP 04009-002, Brazil
Phone: 55-11-5088-3800
Fax: 55-11-5088-3806
Email: sp@happy-science.org
Website: happyscience.com.br

Jundiai

Rua Congo, 447, Jd. Bonfiglioli
Jundiai-CEP, 13207-340
Phone: 55-11-4587-5952
Email: jundiai@happy-science.org

Vancouver

#201-2607 East 49th Avenue
Vancouver, BC, V5S 1J9, Canada
Phone: 1-604-437-7735
Fax: 1-604-437-7764
Email: vancouver@happy-science.org
Website: happy-science.ca

Seoul

74, Sadang-ro 27-gil,
Dongjak-gu, Seoul, Korea
Phone: 82-2-3478-8777
Fax: 82-2-3478-9777
Email: korea@happy-science.org
Website: happyscience-korea.org

Taipei

No. 89, Lane 155, Dunhua N. Road
Songshan District, Taipei City 105, Taiwan
Phone: 886-2-2719-9377
Fax: 886-2-2719-5570
Email: taiwan@happy-science.org
Website: happyscience-tw.org

Malaysia

No 22A, Block 2, Jalil Link Jalan Jalil Jaya 2,
Bukit Jalil 57000, Kuala Lumpur, Malaysia
Phone: 60-3-8998-7877
Fax: 60-3-8998-7977
Email: malaysia@happy-science.org
Website: happyscience.org.my

Nepal

Kathmandu Metropolitan City Ward
No. 15,
Ring Road, Kimdol,
Sitapaila Kathmandu, Nepal
Phone: 97-714-272931
Email: nepal@happy-science.org

Uganda

Plot 877 Rubaga Road, Kampala
P.O. Box 34130, Kampala, Uganda
Phone: 256-79-4682-121
Email: uganda@happy-science.org
Website: happyscience-uganda.org

IMMORTAL HERO

Based on the true story of a man whose near-death experience inspires him to choose life... and change the lives of millions.

41 Awards from 9 Countries!

SPAIN
BARCELONA INTERNATIONAL FILM FESTIVAL 2019 [THE CASTELL AWARDS]

SPAIN
MADRID INTERNATIONAL FILM FESTIVAL 2019 [BEST DIRECTOR OF A FOREIGN LANGUAGE FEATURE FILM]

ITALY
FLORENCE FILM AWARDS JUL 2019 [HONORABLE MENTION: FEATURE FILM]

USA
INDIE VISIONS FILM FESTIVAL JUL 2019 [WINNER (NARRATIVE FEATURE FILM)]

ITALY
FLORENCE FILM AWARDS JUL 2019 [BEST ORIGINAL SCREENPLAY]

ITALY
DIAMOND FILM AWARDS JUL 2019 [WINNER (NARRATIVE FEATURE FILM)]

...and more!

For more information, visit **www.immortal-hero.com**

THE REAL EXORCIST

56 Awards from 9 Countries!

STORY Tokyo —the most mystical city in the world where you find spiritual spots in the most unexpected places. Sayuri works as a part-time waitress at a small coffee shop "Extra" where regular customers enjoy the authentic coffee that the owner brews. Meanwhile, Sayuri uses her supernatural powers to help those who are troubled by spiritual phenomena one after another. Through her special consultations, she touches the hearts of the people and helps them by showing the truths of the invisible world.

USA
GOLD REMI AWARD
53rd WorldFest Houston
International Film Festival 2020

MONACO
BEST FEATURE FILM
17th Angel Film Awards
2020
Monaco International Film Festival

NIGERIA
BEST FEATURE FILM
EKO International Film Festival
2020

THAI
BEST PRODUCTION DESIGN
Thai International Film Festival
2020

...and more!

For more information, visit **www.realexorcistmovie.com**

ABOUT IRH PRESS USA

IRH Press USA Inc. was founded in 2013 as an affiliated firm of IRH Press Co., Ltd. Based in New York, the press publishes books in various categories including spirituality, religion, and self-improvement and publishes books by Ryuho Okawa, the author of over 100 million books sold worldwide. For more information, visit *okawabooks.com*.

Follow us on:

Facebook: Okawa Books   **Twitter:** Okawa Books
Goodreads: Ryuho Okawa   **Instagram:** OkawaBooks
Pinterest: Okawa Books

---- **MEDIA** ----

OKAWA BOOK CLUB

A conversation about Ryuho Okawa's titles, topics ranging from self-help, current affairs, spirituality and religions.

Available at iTunes, Spotify and Amazon Music.

Apple iTunes:
https://podcasts.apple.com/us/podcast/okawa-book-club/id1527893043

Spotify:
https://open.spotify.com/show/09mpgX2iJ6stVm4eBRdo2b

Amazon Music:
https://music.amazon.com/podcasts/7b759f24-ff72-4523-bfee-24f48294998f/Okawa-Book-Club

BOOKS BY RYUHO OKAWA

RYUHO OKAWA'S LAWS SERIES

The Laws Series is an annual volume of books that are mainly comprised of Ryuho Okawa's lectures on various topics that highlight principles and guidelines for the activities of Happy Science every year. *The Laws of the Sun*, the first publication of the laws series, ranked in the annual best-selling list in Japan in 1987. Since then, all of the laws series' titles have ranked in the annual best-selling list for more than two decades, setting socio-cultural trends in Japan and around the world.

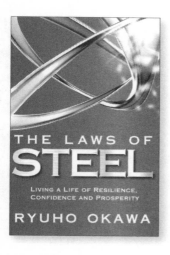

The 26th Laws Series
THE LAWS OF STEEL
LIVING A LIFE OF RESILIENCE, CONFIDENCE AND PROSPERITY

Paperback • 256 pages • $16.95
ISBN: 978-1-942125-65-5

This book is a compilation of six lectures that Ryuho Okawa gave in 2018 and 2019, each containing passionate messages for us to open a brighter future. This powerful and inspiring book will not only show us the ways to achieve true happiness and prosperity, but also the ways to solve many global issues we now face. It presents us with wisdom that is based on a spiritual perspective, and a new design for our future society. Through this book, we can overcome differences in values and create a peaceful world, thereby ushering in a Golden Age.

For a complete list of books, visit **okawabooks.com**

THE TRILOGY

The first three volumes of the Laws Series, *The Laws of the Sun*, *The Golden Laws*, and *The Nine Dimensions* make a trilogy that completes the basic framework of the teachings of God's Truths. *The Laws of the Sun* discusses the structure of God's Laws, *The Golden Laws* expounds on the doctrine of time, and *The Nine Dimensions* reveals the nature of space.

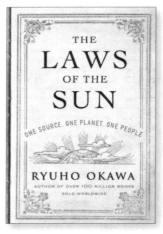

THE LAWS OF THE SUN

ONE SOURCE, ONE PLANET, ONE PEOPLE

Paperback • 288 pages • $15.95
ISBN: 978-1-942125-43-3

IMAGINE IF YOU COULD ASK GOD why He created this world and what spiritual laws He used to shape us— and everything around us. If we could understand His designs and intentions, we could discover what our goals in life should be and whether our actions move us closer to those goals or farther away.

At a young age, a spiritual calling prompted Ryuho Okawa to outline what he innately understood to be universal truths for all humankind. In *The Laws of the Sun*, Okawa outlines these laws of the universe and provides a road map for living one's life with greater purpose and meaning.

In this powerful book, Ryuho Okawa reveals the transcendent nature of consciousness and the secrets of our multidimensional universe and our place in it. By understanding the different stages of love and following the Buddhist Eightfold Path, he believes we can speed up our eternal process of development. *The Laws of the Sun* shows the way to realize true happiness—a happiness that continues from this world through the other.

---

*For a complete list of books, visit **okawabooks.com***

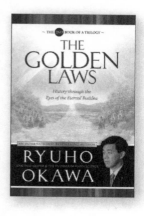

THE GOLDEN LAWS
HISTORY THROUGH THE EYES OF THE ETERNAL BUDDHA

Paperback • 201 pages • $14.95
ISBN: 978-1-941779-81-1

Throughout history, Great Guiding Spirits of Light have been present on Earth in both the East and the West at crucial points in human history to further our spiritual development. *The Golden Laws* reveals how Divine Plan has been unfolding on Earth, and outlines 5,000 years of the secret history of humankind. Once we understand the true course of history, through past, present and into the future, we cannot help but become aware of the significance of our spiritual mission in the present age.

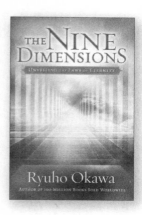

THE NINE DIMENSIONS
UNVEILING THE LAWS OF ETERNITY

Paperback • 168 pages • $15.95
ISBN: 978-0-982698-56-3

This book is a window into the mind of our loving God, who designed this world and the vast, wondrous world of our afterlife as a school with many levels through which our souls learn and grow. When the religions and cultures of the world discover the truth of their common spiritual origin, they will be inspired to accept their differences, come together under faith in God, and build an era of harmony and peaceful progress on Earth.

*For a complete list of books, visit **okawabooks.com***

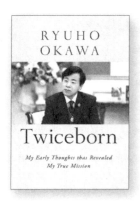

TWICEBORN

MY EARLY THOUGHTS THAT REVEALED MY TRUE MISSION

Paperback • 206 pages • $19.95
ISBN: 978-1-942125-74-7

This semi-autobiography of Ryuho Okawa reveals the origins of his thoughts and how he made up his mind to establish Happy Science to spread the Truth to the world. It also contains the very first grand lecture where he declared himself as El Cantare. The timeless wisdom in *Twiceborn* will surely inspire you and help you fulfill your mission in this lifetime.

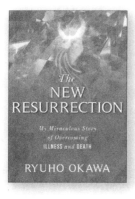

THE NEW RESURRECTION

MY MIRACULOUS STORY OF OVERCOMING ILLNESS AND DEATH

Hardcover • 224 pages • $19.95
ISBN: 978-1-942125-64-8

The New Resurrection is an autobiographical account of an astonishing miracle experienced by author Ryuho Okawa in 2004. This event was adapted into the feature-length film *Immortal Hero*, released in Japan, the United States and Canada during the Fall of 2019. Today, Okawa lives each day with the readiness to die for the Truth and has dedicated his life to selflessly guiding faith seekers towards spiritual development and happiness. The appendix showcases a myriad of accomplishments by Okawa, chronicled after his miraculous resurrection.

*For a complete list of books, visit **okawabooks.com***

THE LAWS OF HAPPINESS

LOVE, WISDOM, SELF-REFLECTION AND PROGRESS

Paperback • 264 pages • $16.95
ISBN: 978-1-942125-70-9

This book endeavors to answer the question, "What is true happiness?" This milestone text introduces four distinct principles, based on the "Laws of Mind" and sourced from Okawa's real-world experience, to guide readers towards sustainable happiness. Okawa's four "Principles of Happiness" present an easy, yet profound framework to ground this rapidly advanced and highly competitive society. In practice, Okawa outlines pragmatic steps to revitalize our ambition to lead a happier and meaningful life.

THE LAWS OF SUCCESS

A SPIRITUAL GUIDE TO TURNING YOUR HOPES INTO REALITY

Paperback • 208 pages • $15.95
ISBN: 978-1-942125-15-0

The Laws of Success offers 8 spiritual principles that, when put to practice in our day-to-day life, will help us attain lasting success and let us experience the fulfillment of living our purpose and the joy of sharing our happiness with many others. The timeless wisdom and practical steps that Ryuho Okawa offers will guide us through any difficulties and problems we may face in life, and serve as guiding principles for living a positive, constructive, and meaningful life.

---

*For a complete list of books, visit **okawabooks.com***

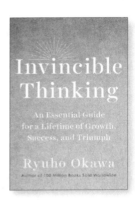

INVINCIBLE THINKING
AN ESSENTIAL GUIDE FOR A LIFETIME OF GROWTH, SUCCESS, AND TRIUMPH

Hardcover • 208 pages • $16.95
ISBN: 978-1-942125-25-9

In this book, Ryuho Okawa lays out the principles of invincible thinking that will allow us to achieve long-lasting triumph. This powerful and unique philosophy is not only about becoming successful or achieving our goal in life, but also about building the foundation of life that becomes the basis of our life-long, lasting success and happiness.

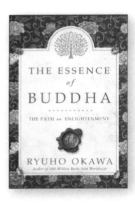

THE ESSENCE OF BUDDHA
THE PATH TO ENLIGHTENMENT

Paperback • 208 pages • $14.95
ISBN: 978-1-942125-06-8

In this book, Ryuho Okawa imparts in simple and accessible language his wisdom about the essence of Shakyamuni Buddha's philosophy of life and enlightenment—teachings that have been inspiring people all over the world for over 2,500 years. By offering a new perspective on core Buddhist thoughts that have long been cloaked in mystique, Okawa brings these teachings to life for modern people. *The Essence of Buddha* distills a way of life that anyone can practice to achieve a life of self-growth, compassionate living, and true happiness.

For a complete list of books, visit **okawabooks.com**

THE LAWS OF INVINCIBLE LEADERSHIP

AN EMPOWERING GUIDE FOR CONTINUOUS AND LASTING SUCCESS IN BUSINESS AND IN LIFE

Hardcover • 224 pages • $19.95
ISBN: 978-1-942125-30-3

Ryuho Okawa shares essential principles for all who wish to become invincible managers and leaders in their fields of work, organizations, societies, and nations. Let Okawa's break-through management philosophy in this empowering guide help you find the seeds of your future success. Your keys to becoming an invincible overall winner in life and in business are just pages away.

THE ROYAL ROAD OF LIFE

BEGINNING YOUR PATH OF INNER PEACE, VIRTUE, AND A LIFE OF PURPOSE

Paperback • 224 pages • $16.95
ISBN: 978-1-942125-53-2

With over 30 years of lectures and teachings spanning diverse topics of faith, self-growth, leadership (and more), Ryuho Okawa presents the profound eastern wisdom that he has cultivated on his approach to life. *The Royal Road of Life* illuminates a path to becoming a person of virtue, whose character and depth will move and inspire others towards the same meaningful destination.

*For a complete list of books, visit **okawabooks.com***

LOVE FOR THE FUTURE
Building One World of Freedom and Democracy Under God's Truth

THE HELL YOU NEVER KNEW
And How to Avoid Going There

WORRY-FREE LIVING
Let Go of Stress and Live in Peace and Happiness

THE CHALLENGE OF THE MIND
An Essential Guide to Buddha's Teachings:
Zen, Karma, and Enlightenment

THE MIRACLE OF MEDITATION
Opening Your Life to Peace, Joy, and the Power Within

MESSAGES FROM HEAVEN
What Jesus, Buddha, Moses, and Muhammad Would Say Today

THINK BIG!
Be Positive and Be Brave to Achieve Your Dreams

THE HEART OF WORK
10 Keys to Living Your Calling

INVITATION TO HAPPINESS
7 Inspirations from Your Inner Angel

---

*For a complete list of books, visit **okawabooks.com***

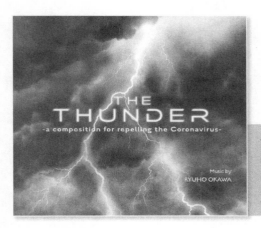

THE EXORCISM

prayer music for
repelling Lost Spirits

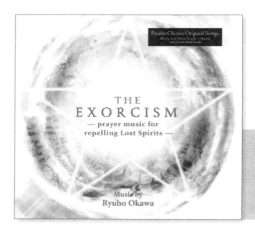

Feel the divine vibrations of this Japanese and Western exorcising symphony to banish all evil possessions you suffer from and to purify your space!

Search on YouTube

the exorcism repelling

for a short ad!

 Available online
Spotify iTunes Amazon